Y LIBRARY

Page to Stage

OXFORD BROOKES
UNIVERSITY
LIBRARY

00 969132 01

Page to Stage

The Craft of Adaptation

Vincent Murphy

The University of Michigan Press
Ann Arbor

ACC. NO.
9691 3201
FUND
EDUG

LOC.
ET
CATEGORY
STAN
PRICE
£24.50

2 4 JAN 2014

CLASS No.
809   MUR

OXFORD BROOKES
UNIVERSITY LIBRARY

Copyright © by the University of Michigan 2013
All rights reserved

This book may not be reproduced, in whole or in part, including
illustrations, in any form (beyond that copying permitted by Sections 107
and 108 of the U.S. Copyright Law and except by reviewers for the public
press), without written permission from the publisher.

Published in the United States of America by
The University of Michigan Press
Manufactured in the United States of America
⊗ Printed on acid-free paper

2016   2015   2014   2013   4   3   2   1

A CIP catalog record for this book is available from the British Library.

Library of Congress Cataloging-in-Publication Data

Murphy, Vincent.
        Page to stage : the craft of adaptation / Vincent Murphy.
             p.   cm.
        Includes bibliographical references and index.
        ISBN 978-0-472-07187-6 (cloth : acid-free paper)—
        ISBN 978-0-472-05187-8 (pbk. : acid-free paper)—
        ISBN 978-0-472-02879-5 (e-book)
        1. Literature—Adaptations—History and criticism.   2. Stage
        adaptations—History and criticism.   I. Title.
        PN171.A33M86   2012
        809—dc23   2012033638

The author dedicates this book to theater artist Ariel Fristoe—for her ongoing brilliance with her internationally acclaimed theater company, Out of Hand, and for being the best daughter he could imagine—and to his grandchildren, Ian Murphy Mednick and Tweed Augusta Fristoe.

Acknowledgments

Special thanks to those great collaborators and friends who helped shape and inspire this book over its decade of gestation, including Karl Squier, John Phillips, William Dillingham, Michael Evenden, Steve Murray, Marilynne McKay, Beth Bornstein, and Alice Benston.

Thanks also to LeAnn Fields, Scott Ham, and Jan Opdyke at the University of Michigan Press; to the anonymous reviewers whose input helped me hone the manuscript; to my developmental editor, Sarah McArthur Smith; to Ellen Gainor, Sandy Thatcher, and Lisa Macklin; to Amy Benson Brown and Elizabeth Gallu of Emory University's Author Development Program; and to the Emory Theater Studies Department. My work in the final stages of the book's creation was also supported in part by a grant from the Emory College of Arts and Sciences and the Laney Graduate School.

Finally, I am especially grateful to my students in the Creating New Works classes at Tufts University, Simon Fraser University, and Emory University for their insights into what works.

Contents

Introduction

This book is about making plays from literature. It is a primer on the art of adaptation. I focus on techniques and strategies you can use to adapt literature into stageworthy plays. To guide you, I have analyzed projects that have been successfully adapted from an array of novels, short stories, poems, autobiographies, and essays, by widely diverse writers.

Both theater professionals and amateurs interested in theater can use the ideas I offer here. I've taught this material for thirty-five years in courses at universities, including Emory, Tufts, Simon Fraser, and the University of Massachusetts. I also lead workshops in adaptation for professional theaters and have even taught it to junior high school students. I hope that those of you with a liberal arts background or who are avid readers will see new possibilities in familiar literature as you read each chapter. You need not be experienced in theater arts to put these ideas into practice; any of you who see creativity as an adventure might be inspired to try your hand at adaptation.

The professionals among you will have a body of experience that gives you your own entry points into what I offer here. As you apply these ideas, you will be able to draw on the techniques you already know, which will allow you to make longer, more daring leaps as you construct your adaptations.

Each adaptor creates his or her own approach for transforming literature into drama. Often the biggest thrill for a theater artist is exploring the unknown, finding something, and then sharing the discovery in a world premier. As maddening as the unknown can be while collaborating with opinionated others, creating theater is the delirious reality of being your own Dr. Frankenstein and Picasso—constructing with found materials something new, beautiful, and alive. This unique inventiveness keeps adaptors returning to the cherished literature we want to bring to life onstage.

Although there are many books on birthing babies, there is not one on birthing a play from a literary source. Some terrific adaptors, including the playwright Horton Foote, director Frank Galati, and actor Simon McBurney, have cogent program notes or articles about their process and philosophy. As I've taught adaptation over the years and experimented with strategies for eclectic subjects and styles of literary sources in my adaptations, it was by trial and error that I uncovered the six basic building blocks that guide me and are central to a successful adaptation. This book is a summary of my discoveries of the methods that most adaptors use, consciously and unconsciously, in the cold heat development of creating something new.

My own discoveries and reading of the limited literature on the subject suggest that these six building blocks are central to a successful adaptation. The building blocks supply a strong, workable model for adapting a wide variety of material from different genres or styles. The strategies are guidelines, not rules. Different adaptors with varying experience and skills, whether in design, acting, directing, music, or movement, or from other disciplines such as psychology or history, will emphasize one element or approach over another.

Artistic endeavors combine fierce imagination and tender logic. Crucial in creativity is finding what feels most vital, what will ground and guide you. These building blocks suggest a possible order. Depending on your material and your connection to it, you may reorder the building blocks to suit yourself. A great character might be your cornerstone, or an evocative theme. Focus on the building block that inspires your best ideas. Then you can return to it and set your other choices with and against it. In creating art we construct with as much planning and clarity as possible, yet we must stay open to the intuitive leaps our imagination and experience give us. Other related theater pieces, films, visual art, music, dance, or experiences in life also influence us and will reveal approaches to your selected adaptation.

The noun *playwright* attests to the construction activity demanded by theater—the idea that a play is *wrighted, crafted, and constructed* rather than just *written*. Playwrights know that many collaborators will be required to bring a work to fruition.

A Brief History of Adaptation

> Adaptation is a profound process, which means you try and
> figure out how to thrive in the world.
> —*The Orchid Thief* in Spike Jonze's film *Adaptation.*

Theater was, in its earliest days, built on adaptation of strictly oral tradition. The biggest context of adaptation is the urge by someone, usually the adaptor, to spread the word and share a really good story that people might have missed in its original form. We told our stories until we learned to enact them. As we evolved, so did the method of telling stories: cave paintings, chants, songs, and epic poems created transformations from one medium into another. That life exists in myriad and exotic forms launched Darwin's *Origin of Species,* which helped creative types like us launch an adaptation industry of narratives morphing into forms and genres that would make the list Polonius spins for Hamlet seem quaint rather than convoluted. A substantive subdiscipline of adaptation studies has been emerging since I started writing this book; its fundamental terms include *intertextuality, intermediality, remediation, translation, appropriation, rewriting, remixing,* and *reloading.* Adaptation got complex and sexy.

The Pyramus and Thisbe play within a play at the end of Shakespeare's *A Midsummer Night's Dream* is an example of a comedic stage adaptation of an ancient Greek myth, once spoken, then later adapted to the page by the Roman poet Ovid in his *Metamorphoses,* and finally enacted on the stage, in new cultures and new styles. Adaptor-director Mary Zimmerman also appropriated and titled her Tony award–winning *Metamorphoses* from the same source. The Bard borrowed from Ovid's *Metamorphoses* a second time when he appropriated the Pyramus and Thisbe story for *Romeo and Juliet.* Centuries later the journey of this adaptation continued when Shakespeare's tragedy morphed into the smash Broadway musical *West Side Story,* and most recently it was reinvented as an Asian gang versus the American mob in the film *Romeo Must Die.*

Charles Dickens was a page-to-stage adaptor of his own work. He went around performing one-man readings from his novels. This, in turn, inspired Patrick Stewart's solo performances of *A Christmas Carol* in London's West End, joining the hundreds of adaptations of *A Christmas Carol* staged all around the world since the novel was published. Adapting Dickens would eventually save the financially strapped Royal Shakespeare Company when it went for broke in adapting *Nicholas Nickleby,* which I write about later in this book.

The prevalence of adaptation in different arts can be witnessed in the eclectic crossbreeding of American designer/adaptor/director/writer Julie Taymor. The art forms, genres, and cultural traditions she cross-pollinates come from painting, dance, music, film, puppetry, theater, performance art, cartoons, mime, fiction and nonfiction, and from cultures as varied as those of Japan, Czechoslovakia, Bali, Peru, America, and India.

A few examples of her adapting range include:

1. Literature to TV: *Hop-Frog* by Edgar A. Poe into *Fool's Fire* on PBS
2. Religious and theatrical enactment of a ritual: *The Haggadah*
3. Literature to musical passion play: *Juan Darian* by Horatio Quiroga
4. Film to stage musical: *The Lion King*
5. Literature to opera: *Grendel* by John Gardner (based on *Beowulf*)
6. Literature to puppet theater: *The Transposed Heads* by Thomas Mann
7. Comic book to film to musical: *Spiderman*
8. Beatles lyrics and songs to film: *Across the Universe*

Who Else Adapts Literature into Scripts?

A hefty proportion of plays has always been adapted from other literature. Four hundred years after Shakespeare adapted Ovid, his namesake theater troupe, the Royal Shakespeare Company, was still at it with *The Life & Adventures of Nicholas Nickleby*. Frank Galati won a Tony award for Best Play when he adapted John Steinbeck's *The Grapes of Wrath,* and I created a literary adaptation from the poetry and prose of William Blake when I was still a teenager. People often turn to the immense body of published literature as a source of material from which to create a play. Theater history's first citation on William Shakespeare is from a frustrated contemporary who ridiculed him by calling him an "Upstart Crow" for using "feathers not his own" (others' stories) as the basis of his plays. But the art of transforming existing stories into popular theater was actually a common practice, then as now. And with no compelling evidence that he actually plagiarized plays or had a ghostwriter other than Hamlet senior, Shakespeare can be counted as one in a long line of playwrights, from classical to contemporary, who have been skillful literary adaptors. Ancient Greek dramatists adapted familiar myths into scripts, giving the characters and stories each playwright's own unique flavor, and the tradition continues through such living writers as Joan Didion, David Hare, David Mamet, Emily Mann, Sarah Ruhl, and Julie Taymor. This distinguished circle waits to welcome you to the adventure of literary adaptation.

Why Adapt Literature for the Stage?

Easily more than a million plays exist. They cover innumerable issues, epochs, characters, places, histories, and affairs. With the wealth of material provided by playwrights, why would we need to turn to literature as the source of a stageworthy play? Are we simply unable to find existing plays that tell the stories or embody the themes and issues vital to us? Let me suggest two major reasons, both common among the actors, directors, writers, producers, artists, and others who find the stage a vibrant place to rediscover their lives.

The first is the powerful content we sometimes find when reading a novel, short story, poem, or essay. A theme, character, storyline, or place may so capture us that we want to share the discovery with others. If theater grew out of the human need to tell our stories, then adaptation takes a story and makes it life-size on the stage, which after your living room is the best place to tell tales. Theater allows us to share a discovered story in the unique way that only live performance can, bringing the storytellers and audience together for the experience.

The second reason to adapt is the challenge of the theatrical form. Each adaptation follows the lead of its sources, but to exist onstage a story must find a new form that has the vitality of life in its immediacy. This challenge often provokes adaptors to find a unique way of telling a story in order to share the experience they had in reading the literature. Breaking the guidelines laid down in Aristotle's plot structure, with its clear beginning, middle, and end, or reinventing the rules of the well-made play, exemplified by the structured nineteenth-century plays of Henrik Ibsen, often leads to exciting new discoveries in the art of playmaking

Adaptors have a range of options when transferring literature from the page to the stage. They can use a largely uncut and barely edited text. They can cut and paste large verbatim sections of the original but leave out other large sections. Or they can create a wholly new version, inspired by the original text yet thoroughly transformed for the stage. In every case, the adaptor's artistic imagination starts by investigating the essential question: is there a play embedded in this novel or short story?

In his lean, dynamic adaptation of *The Grapes of Wrath*, John Steinbeck's searing drama of drought-dispossessed farmers in the 1930s, Frank Galati found the play in the Joad family story and cut much of the novel's rich, descriptive language, replacing it with vivid theatrical imagery.

Fig. 1. *The Cockfighter.* The parents argue in bed after their son loses the cockfight. (Tim Habenger and Joan Croker, PushPush Theater, 1997.)

For this book, my two primary case studies are that *Grapes of Wrath* adaptation and one of my own, constructions from a Frank Manley novel called *The Cockfighter.* Galati used the great symbol of the used car in Steinbeck's book, piled high with the extended family and all their worldly goods, to give the theatrical adaptation an evocative stage image of a homeless yet unified family.

In *The Cockfighter,* a coming-of-age novel, I faced dozens of characters and locations, which made translation to live theater difficult. I ultimately found the embedded play by choosing a thematic approach focused on the legacy of the family. The novel revolves around a twelve-year-old boy who is following in the footsteps of his father—an overbearing, small-time cockfighter. The story explores complex psychological themes, such as the struggle between a mother and father for their child's soul, the oedipal ambivalence of a son toward his father, and the boy's emerging independence. The theme of family bloodline inspired me to focus on the four actual family members in the story: father, son, mother, and outcast uncle. The adaptation focused on the journey of the son as the protagonist, with the others in conflict with him throughout the drama.

I'll examine both the adaptations and the source texts of *The Grapes of Wrath* and *The Cockfighter* in this book, as well as looking at quite a few other plays, some of which may be familiar to you. As these two adaptations reveal, the balancing act in each case is to let the text of the original work lead while finding a stageworthy form in which to tell the story, reveal the characters, develop the theme, and invoke the world of a source. Much like a detective or an archaeologist, each adaptor must sift through the source material for images, ideas, language, and events that will hold the attention of a live audience.

The imagination, which visionary poet William Blake called "the real man . . . which liveth forever," is a crucial part of our being human and of artistic discovery. It culls and develops a complex skill: listening—listening to yourself, to your past and present experiences, and to the material as it ricochets inside your head and heart. That meditative focus conjures images from the material and from connected memories of your own story. Savor these impressions and connections as possible clues when building adaptations.

My Personal Journey as an Adaptor

My first experience of seeing a fully produced play happened when I was thirteen, from backstage at the Boston Children's Theater. My mother's welfare worker had forced me to join BCT after I was almost arrested for using a can to panhandle for money in downtown Boston for a non-existent children's theater. Awkwardly standing backstage at BCT to help with props, I witnessed my teen peers transforming themselves into other characters.

As a child I watched TV shows like *I Love Lucy, Leave It to Beaver,* and *Bonanza* playing out the stories of people who seemed real to me as they got themselves in and out of interesting predicaments. And my previous lack of exposure to live performing arts hadn't kept me from inventing skits with my family and friends or from believing that what we did was like what we saw on television. So once I experienced this transformative power of theater—to alter us, to tell our stories—it took hold of my life and changed it. Since then my career has persistently returned to adapting and directing literary works for the stage.

I first tried my hand at literary adaptation when I helped a high school friend stage Shirley Jackson's short story "The Lottery" for his English class. My performing at the children's theater, often with scripts adapted from Dickens, *Grimm's Fairy Tales,* or *The Arabian Nights,* had given me insight into how to achieve this transformation. I was learning that the challenge of adapting and directing a work from another medium is to find visual imagery and performance vocabularies. That process, once discovered and then rediscovered for particular productions, began to engender a production style with which I could adapt even the heightened, complex language of challenging contemporary writers, to play within the confines of theatrical performance.

Of Heaven and Hell was my first fully produced adaptation for the stage. While still an undergraduate history major at Boston University, I adapted this piece from the writings, graphics, life, and philosophy of William Blake. My success with that first production encouraged me, early in my work as a theater artist, to explore adaptation further and to find and study with professionals who had already developed a sophisticated method of adaptation and ensemble creation.

Within the same year, 1970, I witnessed the acclaimed Open Theater production of *Terminal,* on tour at the Loeb Drama Center at Harvard. From my reading about then current theater trends, I was aware of the groundbreaking work of actor-director Joseph Chaikin and his Open Theater lab but still unprepared for this spare, image-rich production. It got me. *Terminal* upended my previous Stanislavski-based notions of theater, with their mostly realistic-looking characters, places, and relationships. For months I tried to distance myself from the disorienting, emotional, visceral experience this show gave me. I complained to friends about its seemingly limited use of a character's through-line or its lack of a relationship I could recognize, such as father and son. Trying to make sense of what I had seen, I finally started researching the artist's techniques and philosophy. In Joseph Chaikin's *The Presence of the Actor* and books on the Open Theater, I uncovered ideas and methodologies of collaborative creation that continue to inform my work today, almost forty years later.

So, from the beginning of my career, I was asking questions about how to adapt literature and developing processes for answering those questions. These, in turn, have become the abiding questions and processes that have shaped my subsequent work, since a significant proportion of my professional theater productions as a director, producer, designer, dramaturge, and actor have been adaptations from literature, many of them adaptations that I have written. (See the appendix for a full list.)

My frustration with the scarcity of good new plays, coupled with the often formulaic approach to playwriting, has led me to explore non-theatrical texts that have a vivid voice: stories that speak to the moment and the imagination. These nontheatrical texts create a challenge, and answering that challenge has become a cornerstone of my work. The innovative, nontheatrical writing of contemporary authors, including James Baldwin, John Barth, Samuel Beckett, Athol Fugard, Shirley Jackson, Anne Sexton, and Wole Soyinka, has inspired adaptations that remain the most rewarding and challenging products of my career as a theater artist. (I explore the details of the process I used to create some of these works in chapter 7, "Balancing the Blocks.")

Frank Manley often adapted his own short stories into plays, but he believed that his novel, *The Cockfighter*, would be impossible to adapt for the stage. He could not picture it staged because he could imagine the cockfighting he had described in the novel only literally, as one could film it with real birds. For the stage the only option he could see in his mind's eye was definitely unworkable: actors in chicken suits fighting it out. I knew from adapting the literature of several other challenging writers that the cockfight could be represented in other ways. Solving this dilemma for *The Cockfighter*, like challenges with other adaptations, gave me new perspective on all six building blocks. As you will see from reading about that process, a key guide that I have found for envisioning an adaptation is in building block 4: finding a stageable image—a visual representation that grounds the theme in the space and manifests a key metaphor in a playable way onstage. Choosing the key image of a cock-fighting ring, I was able to suggest the multiple locations and distill the dozens of characters in *The Cockfighter* down to the essentials for a stage version of the novel.

The excitement of adaptation is having wonderful source material to help sustain one's creativity. South African playwright Athol Fugard speaks eloquently of his lifelong fear of facing a blank page when he writes. The adaptor, however, can return to the pages of the original novel, short story, or poem if inspiration wanes. With literature that inspires me, I have a companion of the best sort, one that I can go deeper with, be surprised by, be enticed to ask essential questions of, and interact with for revealing answers. If the unexamined life might not be worth living, then the examined novel we cherish becomes a deep dive into characters, themes, and places that nourish our souls and open up the opportunity to create a work of art inspired by another.

The Six Building Blocks

Chapters 1 through 6 are dedicated to the six building blocks, providing detailed examples and construction tips to aid you in developing your own adaptation. Blocks 1, 3, and 5 are content elements: they define what your story is about. They are your building materials. Blocks 2, 4, and 6 are performance vocabularies: they decide how you tell that story. They are your tools for shaping the material. Here is a brief summary of each building block:

1. Find literature that compels you and define its theme.

You will work on your adaptation for weeks or months, and you will likely be involved in the rehearsal process to produce it. Artistic creation is an act requiring not only talent but also stamina, and you want to be working on material that will nourish your enthusiasm for that process. One paradox inherent in the act of creation for performance is the necessity of making a large work graspable in manageable, stageable terms. Knowing what your connection is to the piece, as well as its relevance for your audience, will guide your choices about what to include in the adaptation script.

In chapter 1, which deals with building block 1, you will learn how to choose wisely to sustain your passion, how to reread your choice to help you clarify your formal understanding of the work, and how to hone your perception of the intuitive or emotional responses that will shape the adaptation by naming your one major theme. You will learn how to use clues from each of the other building blocks to choose a theme that works for practical application.

2. Select passages to create a template for your script.

The work of adaptation is about mining your source for playable scenes and language. You need to find the most promising passages from your original material and learn how to spot what can be best used as is and what may need more editing or transformation to work for your play.

In chapter 2, on building block 2, you will highlight the dialogue and narrative from your source material that seems most evocative to you. You will cut and paste your most promising scenes together into a rough cut of your script. And you will learn ways to use existing dialogue from your original story, as well as how you can create monologues and dialogues from narrative passages.

3. Identify the principal characters and relationships for your adaptation.

You must decide who your main focus is in telling the story. The choice may be obvious from your original material, or it may not. What makes creation simultaneously exciting and frightening is that you get to play God, deciding who is important and why. And once you know your main characters, you get to choose which of the relationships are most important for you to explore.

Building block 3, in chapter 3, will help you choose the most important characters in the story you want to tell and determine what relationship they have that best reveals the conflict of the adaptation. Using the scenes you have already chosen as a guide, you will get to know your characters and start to make choices that will flesh them out thoroughly.

4. Choose an evocative, stageable image.

Theater exists in a three-dimensional space. To move a story from the page to the stage, you must imagine where the event is happening onstage. Theater does not race from one literal location to another like a reader's imagination or a film viewer's eye. Rather, as actor and audience stay present together in one space, a theater production and its audience's imagination transform that space to suit the needs of the story.

Building block 4, in chapter 4, will explore how to balance the realistic and the imagined by finding a visual vocabulary. Since theater functions best in a stage environment suggested by both the theme and the metaphorical space in which the event will take place, I will share examples of creative ways in which adaptors have used visual images from their source stories to define location and resonant visual details.

5. State the storyline.

By letting your chosen theme drive your decisions about what to include, and by focusing on one character or relationship, you force yourself to build a spine based on one simple storyline, which becomes the backbone of the work.

In chapter 5, building block 5 will help you to define the storyline that is emerging from the scenes you are choosing to include in your adaptation. You will learn what role conflict plays in your plot, as well as how to identify what prior history is essential to include in your script. And you will clarify how to find the central event of the play and each scene.

6. Craft playable actions.

The essence of theater, what makes it distinct from other forms of art, is performance—actors performing actions. You need to know how to recognize an action and determine whether or not your scenes include actions.

In chapter 6, building block 6 will build on what you have learned about actions in the earlier chapters on language, character, and storyline to help you identify the key actions of your scenes. You will check to see that your central events are truly actions, and you will learn to look for opportunities to include pure physical action in your script, via stage directions.

Each of the building blocks is your contribution to the remarkable collaboration that is a theater production. Selecting a story with a resonant, clear theme (building block 1) will provide a solid starting place for everyone involved in a production of your adaptation, especially a dramaturge. By sorting through the original language (building block 2) to choose best material, you are doing your job as adaptor-playwright to create the script. By paying attention to each of these other elements as you create the text for the other artists to work with, you find ways to feed each of them in their individual talents: the actors with character (building block 3), the designer with image (building block 4), and the director with storyline (building block 5). A clear sequence of defining actions (building block 6) will feed everyone involved in bringing the piece to life. A beautifully finished script will give your producer a clear beginning for the work of assembling the artists to stage the play. Part of the task of this book is to give you just enough understanding of what these fellow artists need so that you can create a script that inspires each of them and stimulates their unique creative contributions to the production.

Balancing the Blocks

After you work your way through the six building block chapters that comprise Part One, doing the Construction Exercises as you go, you will have a full-length script draft. Part Two offers three additional chapters to help you finish your work and understand the adaptation process. The first, chapter 7, "Balancing the Blocks," guides you to check for sturdy construction in your script. You will learn how to find the right balance between the building blocks—the mix that best suits your particular material. You'll decide what your driving content is and which performance vocabulary you rely on most. And, for this final step of creating your adaptation, you will also evaluate how well you are handling the transitions within and between scenes. Using Construction Exercises like those in the six building block chapters, you'll finish a script to be ready to share with collaborators.

The two remaining chapters illustrate how collaboration can work, as chapter 8 shares case studies of two works I have adapted and chapter 9 looks at the work of master adaptors, who provide models of ways that adaptations can be created and produced.

Throughout the book, to illustrate the process of transforming a work of literature into a play, I offer examples from a wide range of sources. In particular, I use my adaptation of *The Cockfighter* as the primary source of examples and comparisons. If you want to familiarize yourself with the overall storyline and see what the completed script looks like, it is available in the play collection *Humana Festival '99*. Beyond *The Cockfighter*, I will be using examples from the other adaptations I've created in the hope that glimpses into details of the process will illuminate your understanding of the various ways in which this creative process can work. I'll also refer to the work of other adaptors. Given many readers' familiarity with Steinbeck's novel *The Grapes of Wrath* and the success of Frank Galati's adaptation of it, I have used it to illustrate key ideas. Shakespeare, too, considering the familiarity with his stories and the excellence of his craftsmanship, proves a useful touchstone for illustrating key aspects of play structure that you will need to know as an adaptor. And I occasionally reference adaptations for other media, such as film or radio, in the hope that you will be inspired to branch out.

As you work through the chapters, you will be asked to select a literary work to adapt for the stage and to use the building blocks to produce a script by the time you finish the book. Have fun in your process of exploration and discovery. Recognizing what inspired you in the original literary work, attempt to develop a script that will share its essential elements with others.

After completing the exercises in this book, you should be able to accomplish the following:

- Unearth the play latent in favorite fictions
- Know the difference between literature and theater
- Deduce what the basic story is
- Build a play around a favorite character
- Understand dramatic structure
- Grasp how relationships and conflicts fuel drama
- Imagine a theatrical environment
- Know the building blocks of a play

After you have used the steps and applied them to your own process of adaptation, you will be able to find characters that move you and then take apart their story and rebuild it as a play. As you bring your favorite stories to life and create three-dimensional characters from literature, you'll get to shape these characters' lives in whatever way works for your piece. You may conjure up new ways to tell stories. Best of all, as you create your new work, you will have the privilege of partnering with the work of a fiction writer you love.

Part One

The Six Building Blocks

1 ✦ *Building Block One*

Find Literature That Compels You and Define Its Theme

We carry stories with us, beginning with the tales read to us in infancy. We wrote novice reports in junior high school on *Silas Marner, The Color Purple,* or *Catcher in the Rye.* These stories were all prologue for the fiction, nonfiction, poetry, *New Yorker* articles, and other reading we've done since. And anyone reading this book, with or without theater experience, can use a ready imagination to adapt a favorite piece of literature for the stage. When a particular story enthralls us, we can look to the stage as a place to share what engaged us.

Choosing literature for adaptation is first about a strong connection to your building materials. While still a liberal arts undergraduate, I first encountered William Blake and found the dichotomies of life that are so present to a nineteen-year-old vividly expressed in his two-hundred-year-old prose, poetry, and art. His *Songs of Innocence and Experience* and his evocations of heaven and hell prompted me to cull from the canon of his work a two-hour theatrical event. In subsequent decades, powerful writing by James Baldwin on the nature of race; Michael Ondaatje's brilliant, image-rich evocation of Billy the Kid and the American West; and the despairing beauty of Samuel Beckett's fiction each challenged me to find a home for them on the stage.

We read literature first for the pleasure of discovery. Reading is a wonderful and solitary experience, as we find literature that engages our imaginations, emotions, and realities. The joy of anticipating the next Harry Potter installment was, for many, a waiting for the quiet pleasure of entering a world both familiar and fantastic. One's imagination plunges into a pool of fascinating characters, real and improbable places, and an array of desires, fears, and possibilities that we also face in our own lives.

Interestingly, the reviews of the early Potter films critiqued the too-literal translation of the books into film. The pleasure of adapting into another medium, like the pleasure of reading itself, is in the permission you have to engage your own imagination and experience with the art at hand, in making manifest those personal discoveries.

Ways to Think about Choosing Material

Joseph Chaikin, the legendary founder of the Open Theater, once gave an amusing analogy for the consequences of making choices lightly. During a winter workshop in New York City, he explained that choosing material that only "interests" you—whether to adapt, act, or direct—is like kissing someone you merely "like." Your involvement and returns only diminish each time you return to the material, as the choice lacks passion, connection, and a future. When you choose material that you feel passion for, it's like the thrill of playing sports, making love, or learning something revelatory. You are both within the experience and sensing it from the outside, in an ecstatic connection. You hunger to go further, to probe deeper, to open up to what you already know, as well as to the unknown.

Frank Galati has successfully adapted stage plays not only from John Steinbeck but also from literary sources as diverse as William Faulkner, Gertrude Stein, and Vladimir Nabokov. He received an Academy Award nomination for his film adaptation of Anne Tyler's *The Accidental Tourist*. Talking about adaptation in an interview for *American Theatre* magazine, he emphasized the importance of the quality of his source material: "If one is to be lucky in the task of adaptation, first find a novel that has a real play in it, for it's not so much the skill of the adapter as the skill of the novelist that creates the success" (20).

Horton Foote, a playwright and adaptor for more than one medium, has described his process for choosing adaptation material this way: "To be really successful adapting, one must like the original work. I don't have to always understand it, but I have to like it and be willing to try to understand it and go through the painful process of entering someone else's creative world" (7). Discussing "The Displaced Person," a Flannery O'Connor story he adapted for the *American Short Story* series on the television show *Playhouse 90*, Foote talks about how his entry point is specific to each piece: "For this one, it was the characters that intrigued me most and proved wonderfully comic companions in my stay in the O'Connor country" (8). Most important: "There is only one rule I'm sure of. Do something you really admire" (20).

Simon McBurney, actor and acclaimed artistic director of several theatrical adaptations for Britain's Théatre de Complicité, has also given us a window into his selection process: "I'm not attracted to literary, narrative, or prose work as an idea. I became interested in a particular subject matter. And there will be urgent concerns, urgent ideas, urgent stories within my own life. There is no formula. The desire to take a work of prose is, you suddenly have a desire to make it present."

What is essential for you as an adaptor is to feel that desire to make it present. You can't always know all the reasons why a particular story compels you, but you need to connect with the piece. And the effort to articulate why you do connect with it will often point you toward the best place to start your work as an adaptor.

Discovering Your Theme

To find the play in the literary source, you need to decide what it is about. What idea fascinates you? This theme will be the foundation of your adaptation. It is the metaphoric floor to which you will add the walls, roof, and various rooms, that is, the characters, language, settings, and conflicts, to build a satisfying adaptation. In the writing and subsequently in the production, how an adaptor and then collaborating theater artists follow through on a theme decides what a play is about. While there may be several themes, the adaptor is charged with finding and dramatizing the one that best evokes the story.

There are dozens of adaptations of Charles Dickens's *A Christmas Carol*. Those most resonant with the original novel focus on Scrooge's redemptive transformation, a spiritual and socioeconomic journey into his past. From Atlanta to London, I've walked out of reductive versions in which the adaptation got lost in special effects and exotic characterizations. Losing sight of the theme negates the focus on Scrooge's true journey and the redemptive power of his transformation.

Theater responds to the present moment more fully than any other art form. Often theater is the first art form attacked in repressive political situations due to its ability to put words and body—a human face—to the protest. Theater lives in the political farces of Dario Fo, the histories of Shakespeare, the street theater of El Teatro Campesino. It lives in Samuel Beckett's woman buried up to her neck in his play *Happy Days* or in the husband's desires for his wife in his short story "Enough." Both pieces by Beckett work because he knows how to share his story with an audience hungry for knowledge and experience. The success of your adaptation depends on finding that kind of connection.

What often compels you relates to either personal or social issues you feel vexed with at a given moment. This might be an ongoing sense in your life of feeling conflicted or thinking in two contradictory ways about something that matters, such as marriage, worthy careers, or true friendship. The duality found in National Book Award winner John Barth's plaintive short story "Petition" explores that double, schizophrenic sense in the story of Siamese twins joined chest-to-back: the back brother delicate and introspective, the front hedonistic and explosive.

Respect the intelligence, needs, and imagination of the audience as if they are friends and family invited to your metaphoric campfire to share the tale. To make your material relevant, keep in mind the place in which you live, because your task will be to connect the story to what your society finds vital. You should please yourself first: you are the society in microcosm, so pay close attention to your observations as you contemplate what affects you.

Your main theme helps flesh out and counterpoint the story. When you've decided on a theme that is evocative and resonates with the text you've chosen, say it out loud, then close your eyes and watch which moments from the source material come up in your memory and imagination. You know you are onto a vibrant theme when at least three vivid moments come to mind. (My rule of three in the arts is that a critical mass is achieved when you discover three good examples of what you are searching for, including themes, a character trait, a major conflict, or the nature of a relationship.)

Naming Your Theme

There are two ways to think about naming your theme. The first is a word or phrase that names an idea: *transformation, loss, passion, chaos.* It may be a word that comes up explicitly in your original text or an implicit idea that strikes you as important as you read. You may arrive at this word by noticing your characters' qualities: *desperation, ambition, honesty, duplicity.* Relationships could cue you: *clinging, loyalty, domination, playfulness.* Or your characters' actions may give you a vital theme: *dancing, hunting, embracing, sniping.* Images in your material could spark a theme idea:

Fig. 2. *Dreaming with an AIDS Patient.* Multiple aspects of the dreamer meet. (Andrew McIlroy, Buck Newman Jr., Judge Luckey, Peter Greenberg, Greg Hall, Susan Jacobs, Jennifer Langsam, Theresa O'Shea, and Jason Rappaport, Theater Emory, 1990.)

collapse, from a collapsing house; or *peace,* from the peacefulness of your character's secret retreat.

Once you have a word or phrase that defines your theme, the second way to articulate it is in a sentence or question. Give your theme idea a context: what happens to this idea in your story? You can create a question to which your story explores a possible answer: "Where does relentless ambition lead?" or "What is loyalty?" in a story with characters whose actions offer two different, competing versions of an answer to that question. Or if you see your adaptation's verdict on this theme as clear, you can state it in a declarative sentence: "Relentless ambition reaps loneliness and loss." As you begin the work of your adaptation, start with at least one question. By the time you finish drafting your script, you may have an answering sentence.

The strong foundation of theme allows you, your fellow artists, and your audience to move horizontally and vertically through the expanse of the story. That is, you can build a sturdy framework of plot from your source with a strong theme. You can build the spaces that your characters travel through. With a clear theme you will have a solid floor as you define the visual, spatial elements of your production that guide you in constructing the roof and rooms of your adaptation with the related materials of character, place, conflict, and relationships. Your main theme allows you to delve into other, related themes that intersect with your main idea.

Considering Your Landscape and Neighborhood

You may come to this book already knowing what you want to adapt. Perhaps you have already found a story that leaps off the page. Or you may be working within other parameters. An organization or a teacher may have asked you to choose material for an adaptation. To be successful in building a clear story, your adaptation has to take the following key external factors into account.

Why are you doing the adaptation?

As you discover novels and short stories that feel captivating enough to adapt, the bedrock consideration about working on your adaptation is whether or not you feel a compelling reason to tell its story onstage. You need at least one vivid connection to the language, a character, a place, or a relationship that you can imagine in a three-dimensional space.

My first example of connecting to literature and adapting it happened in 1967, at the height of the Vietnam War. For an English class assignment, my high school friends and I adapted into a short theater piece Shirley Jackson's "The Lottery," a story about ordinary human beings' inherent violence. We seized on the story and the image of a baby carriage as a link to compelling current events witnessed each evening on the news. We outlined a play, improvised the dialogue, and set out a baby carriage to be stored facing upstage, away from the audience. What fascinated and hit us with horror was the story's ability to help make sense of the many atrocities being reported from the war. The inhuman trait of seeing those not like us as objects and the hysteria embedded in mob rule were clues to the infamous documented atrocities of the village of My Lai, where Lt. William Calley and his squad of American troops slaughtered innocent families.

If your source story is assigned rather than chosen, the challenge is to find your personal and topical connection to the material. You will use the construction exercises to look for those connection points.

But if you do have the freedom to choose your own material, then your task as you read potential texts is to stay alert to themes that are of personal importance to you.

Who is your intended audience?

At times you are the audience: you write to make discoveries and to please yourself. Occasionally you have specific audiences.

Black Witness, my adaptation of material by African American novelist and social critic James Baldwin, was created for people in Boston who were trying to make sense of a local, in-the-headlines murder. Inbred racism had persuaded them to blame a black man for the murder of a white woman, who was ultimately found to have been killed by her white husband, who had accused the black man of the crime.

My adaptation of *Crow*, former British poet laureate Ted Hughes's beautifully bleak apocalyptic poems, was staged to mark the arrival of his archives at Emory University's Manuscript, Archives and Rare Book Library and the opening of the grand Schwartz Performing Arts Center. Consider who will see your piece and let that shape the way you connect with the material and, therefore, with the audience.

Where is your adaptation likely to be produced—in what kind of space?

Seeing theater in a variety of spaces—proscenium, blackbox, found spaces—guides your intuition toward a possible place for staging your adaptation. As you finalize your selection, begin to envision some of your choices as an adaptor. Consider how you can pare down the original material. For your play to work, you will need to be able to scale the material to a live theater space.

Although naturalism and kitchen-sink realism can be powerful styles in which to tell a story, adapting literature often calls on us to think outside the accepted conventions of place, time, and character. Whereas film tries to signal a change in location—from Boston in one moment to Atlanta the next—with visual cues (perhaps from footage actually shot in those two cities), and fiction can simply tell the reader that the action has shifted to a new location, theater finds more visceral ways to represent that shift. For instance, an actor who remains physically present through the transition from one scene to the next can shift from a northern accent to a southern one right in front of you, thereby signaling the change of scene.

What copyright restrictions, if any, are you working within?

After seventy-five years, most literature loses its copyright protections and enters the public domain. Texts can then be cut, reordered, and added to, without permission of the original author. Copyright laws can be complex, so doing a little research into the relevant rules for your chosen original material is a good idea and may even force you to make a different choice. Material still under copyright restriction must be cleared with authors or their representatives before an adaptation can be performed. One typically gets in touch with the author's agent or publisher, but if you can reach the author directly, you may have a better chance of successfully pitching your ideas and passion for the work.

Institutions such as universities or nonprofit theaters are often given limited-use options for adaptations. As a condition of receiving permission to adapt the piece, the adaptor agrees to restrict the performances to the host theater or a short-term run.

How I Choose Material to Adapt

I had the unique opportunity to read an early draft of Frank Manley's novel *The Cockfighter* a few years before it was published. I am always on the lookout for adaptable material when I read, and I had previously workshopped and directed premiers of plays he had written. After reading it to give Manley some feedback, I found myself haunted by this story of a southern boy at puberty caught in a tug-of-war between his parents. Whenever a story captures me this way, I begin to investigate its theatrical possibilities. The climactic scene depicts the boy handling his father's prize-winning bird in a to-the-death championship match.

In the story of *The Cockfighter*, the protagonist, Sonny, is, at age twelve and a half, on the verge of becoming a man, but in his mother's eyes he is still a naive little boy. Everything changes when his father, Jake Cantrell, owner of the Snake Nation Cock Farm, presents him with his own rooster, a gray that the boy calls Lion. A three-time winner worth nearly four thousand dollars, the bird becomes the pet Sonny always wanted. But cockfighting is not for pets, or children. Sonny quickly comes to love Lion but is soon faced with the biggest decision of his life, one that will drive him into deep moral conflict and ultimately change him forever. Rebelling against his father's demands, Sonny chooses his own way, preserving his integrity and drawing on the courage, fierceness, and determination that he reveres in Lion. He steps into manhood by facing the frightening consequences of his actions.

Manley, though himself an accomplished writer of plays, as well as fiction, couldn't see the novel as a play. The enormous challenge of evoking the cockfighting pit seemed to him better suited to its imaginative realm of fiction or to the literalizing medium of film. Warned, daunted, yet still captured by Sonny's complex psychological struggle to become like his mother or father (a struggle many of us face in life), I felt compelled to proceed with this adaptation. I reread the novel three times, highlighting dialogue and the narration that carried the story forward and evoked the cockfighting world. The resulting adaptation is an example of the cut-and-paste technique of approaching a novel in which the theme, dialogue, and narration were a guide to the adaptation.

In the rest of this chapter, I will use *The Cockfighter* to demonstrate how any of the elements of your source material—any of the building blocks—can lead you back to the fundamental task that is building block 1: finding your material and naming your theme. As the first example will show, you may discover your choice directly, simply by having a strong response to the themes in the potential source material. But you may have a powerful reaction to other specific elements—a character, or the language, or an image, each the focus of another building block—which connect you to the potential source material, make you want to choose it, and point toward a theme.

Examples of Passages That Captured Me (Building Block 1)

As I read and reread the novel, I connected with certain passages, and they pointed me toward theme ideas. What follows are some of the key sections that caught my attention. It was the dialogue I have marked in boldface that gave me the most specific clues.

The boy existing between the worlds of mother and father, of women and men:

> If she'd had her way, he'd be a girl.
>   That's what his daddy told him one time.
>   She always wanted one, he said.
>   The boy asked him, How come?
>   And his daddy said, well, she don't like men.
>   He laughed and said, Except me. She likes me all right. That's how come she married me. But she don't like the general run of them. They're too rough.
>   And the boy said, What about me?
>   And his daddy said, You aren't a man. I'm talking about men. I'm not talking about little children. They're all pretty much the same when they're little, girls and boys both, until they grow up. Then they get different. And I don't mean between the legs. I mean up here—and he tapped his head. Their thinking's all screwed up. You're going to have to wait a while. **You're still something in between**. (23)

The mother wishing she could envelop her son:

> She didn't know that if she had a boy and he lived to grow up, her husband would come and take him away from her, and by the time he was fifteen or sixteen, she wouldn't be able to tell them apart. She might as well not even have had him. Might as well plant him in a flowerpot as far as she was concerned.
>   If it had been a girl, she wouldn't have cared. A daughter would have been hers for the rest of her life. **But if it was a boy, and she really loved him, she had to let him become what he was.** And that's what hurt her so much now. She loved him so much that **she had to let go and lose him.** And not just now. She had to do it over and over the rest of her life. (55)

The boy existing between the worlds of boyhood and manhood:

"A twelve-year-old boy handling a champion—"
    "Thirteen," the boy said, interrupting him.
    "You thirteen?"
    "Just about."
    "Just about's not it. I'm going to say twelve. That sounds better. That's going to attract a lot of attention. Folks going to want to bet on that." (63)

The father's forcing his son's rite of passage when he discards the son as a loser:

He gave the bird back to the boy.
    "Go on and fight him," he said.
    "What's going to happen?"
    "He's going to lose. He's got the white head. I never heard of one like that winning."
    "What do I do?"
    "The best you can. That's all you can do."
    "They going to kill him?"
    "Damn right, they're going to kill him—a Goddamn, fucking champion bird." . . .
    "There's no help for it. People and cocks are a lot alike in a lot of different ways, and dying's one of them. I don't care how game they are, it's going to happen sooner or later, and the best thing to do is to go off and leave them and get on with the rest of your life. I'm going back up there. There're some folks I was with," and he turned and went back to the bleachers.
    "I'll fight him for you," the boy said, calling after him. "He's going to win. I'm going to make him." (114–16)

The highlighted dialogue also added weight to my emerging theme of an unformed boy coming to a sense of self and his destiny by identifying with his bird. The dialogue reveals the gender tension in the culture and how it influences and infects the child in this family.

Examples of Lucid and Evocative Language (Building Block 2)

The language in the following passages took me inside the echo chambers of my own head, reminding me what families sound like.

In the first of these four passages, the father's language sounds like a drumbeat, as he insists on his own point of view:

> "He had a hard time," his momma said.
> "Don't give me that, Lily. I had a hard time. You had a hard time. We all had a hard time. That's how it is. As long as you're alive, you're going to have a hard time. The only time you're not is when you're dead, and he's working on that. He's working on that every chance he got." (191–92; see also the script, 150)

The mother offers a counterpoint, conciliatory and evasive:

> "I told you. He's just a boy. You shouldn't have trusted him."
> "I didn't trust him. I didn't trust him any more than I trusted that brother of yours. Neither one of them got any sense. I got to do all their thinking for them, and that wears me out. I get tired sometimes."
> "I know you do."
> "I get tired, Lily. It wears me out, and I get discouraged. I'm discouraged right now." (192)

The following passage shows off Manley's gift for articulating a pregnant woman's sensual inner life, as she ponders the child growing inside her:

> It would be hers. And it would always be with her—flesh of her flesh, bone of her bone. She imagined the great, sheltering wings of her pelvis closing around it, like valves of stone, protecting it from all harm until they became one thing—one man and one woman, one husband and one wife, one mother and one child—one woman, one son. (58)

In contrast the father's blunt, ugly language conjures images that are both funny and emasculating of his son as he commingles sex and violence:

"Get away from that cock, like I said. You don't want to get them used to you. Standing there with your thumb up your ass looking at them like it was a girl showing her tits, they turn into chickens." (38)

Examples of Unforgettable Characters and Relationships (Building Block 3)

Feeling empathetic with the characters you meet in a story is promising. Characters that are multilayered and surprising offer the strongest potential for adaptation. I found several characters who engaged me in *The Cockfighter*.

- The boy, Sonny: impressionable, loving, mocking, facing a rite of passage
- The father, Jake: crude, funny, sexual
- The mother, Lily: tender, reserved, feisty

And the relationships between the characters gave them throughlines, which held my attention from the beginning of the story all the way to the end.

- Lily envelops Sonny; he breaks away.
- Jake trains Sonny to be disciplined and cold; Sonny creates a secret, tender world.

Examples of Evocative Images that Might Be Stageable (Building Block 4)

My personal first impressions are often visual images. While reading *The Cockfighter*, I noticed in the text or was reminded of images from my own experience: beads of light, taut stillness, thin walls, witnessing a cockfight in Bali, a blizzard of feathers, cages, handling, cold, blue light, sheltering wings. These images stood out as visceral discoveries that connected me to this material and promised to inspire my imagination as I built my adaptation. If you have found the piece that will sustain your passion for it, your imagination immediately begins to envision flashes of the adaptation: colors, the claustrophobic quality of hiding in a small compartment, bodies moving like ballet in the backyard, the low sigh of a satisfied child, the intense mouthing of what you fear.

Example of an Involving Storyline (Building Block 5)

Noting Sonny's development through the story, I knew that my theme would involve his relationship and maturation in the context of his family. I began to realize that it would focus on the boy's rite of passage to a self. This building-block clue for discerning the theme comes from listing the important events in the central character's movement through the entire story. For Sonny, they are that he

- Develops a secret life with Lion
- Rejects his mom by tossing away her sandwich
- Emulates his father by humiliating his Uncle Homer
- Lets the wounded Lion fight until it dies
- Realizes that his father sees him as a loser
- Slaughters his father's cocks

From these events I added more clues to finding the theme. The events build from his rejection of the mother's influence to his rejection of the father's when Sonny goes his own way toward the final confrontation with the cocks. Further defining the idea of the theme, I decided that the boy's rite of passage is to reject both his parents and find his own way.

Example of Envisioning Playable Actions (Building Block 6)

As I read the novel the first few times, visceral actions would occur to me that seemed worthy of staging. When a character "handled" a bird during the preparation for a fight derby, I imagined a gentle cradling. When the dad grunted and his son imitated, I began to envision a pattern of imitated movements between these two actors. When mom talked of "sheltering wings," I saw enfolding gestures that then had her arms lifting a flower print nightgown over her head to reveal another character. The constant eye imagery could become lighting involving spots and blinking bulbs. And "wring his neck" conjured specific hand gestures for the brutal dad, the ineffectual Homer, and the compassionate son.

Examples of Research That Informs Your Understanding of the Theme

Research can be useful in conjunction with any of the building blocks. In fleshing out my understanding of the theme of *The Cockfighter,* I found critical reviews of the novel that offered useful insights into the text. Astute critics often write distilled storylines to describe a book, cite themes they find crucial, and give additional clarity about character, place, plot, and style of language. Reviewer Sudip Bose wrote of *The Cockfighter,* "Among other things, this book is about Jake's abandonment of Sonny, an innocent boy who wishes more than anything to become like his father." And *Publishers Weekly* wrote, "Manley captures the volatile thoughts and feelings of a 12-year-old boy as the young hero of this spare, suspenseful debut steps outside of the shelter of his mother's care and into his father's arena."

Biographical information about the author can also spark ideas or clarify your take on the work you are choosing, as can other works by the same writer.

✦ ✦ ✦ ✦

CONSTRUCTION EXERCISES FOR BUILDING BLOCK 1

That a piece of literature is beautifully written and has great characters, locations, relationships, and conflicts is not enough to make it come alive onstage. Your work as an adaptor will decide whether a stageworthy play emerges. The following exercises can help you solidify your choice of material and articulate your connection with its theme, and they will lay the foundation for your work with the other building blocks.

To clarify what compels you about the literature you are considering for adaptation, you will reread your choice three times, then articulate what you've found. These multiple readings are for the pleasure of rediscovering the story and for beginning to notice the nuances of the characters, plot, structure, and language. It's courting the source, getting to know its feel, rhythm, and idiosyncrasies. And if it feels like kissing someone you are attracted to, then you know you want to go further and stay involved.

   A. Get a copy of the text that you can mark up. As you reread, underline and make margin notes, mark passages that get to you. What do you connect to, at a visceral level? Mark words or sections that articulate themes of the story, character traits, and key locations. Keep a notepad for your intuitive connections and subjective responses. Notice your feelings as you read. Jot down phrases or images that come to you.

   B. After the repeated readings, reflect on what you've read. Scan your text markings and notes to see what jumps out at you. Is there anything that recurs regularly, such as a word or references to a certain character? Were you particularly struck by a climactic scene? Is there an idea that you want to explore? Freewrite a few paragraphs for yourself or do a journal entry.

   C. Using the following list, which is based on the six building blocks in this book, define the key elements of the story that will become your building blocks if you choose this piece. If there is one for which you can't yet answer the questions, leave it for last.

      1. Personal Connection and Theme. What were your first impressions of this story?
         What makes this story important to tell now?
         Name the main theme idea that intrigues you. Frame it as a sentence or a question.

      2. Language. Cite three paragraphs of evocative narrative prose.
         Cite six lines of dialogue that capture you.
         Speak these passages out loud to see how much you favor them as language for performance.

      3. Characters. List the main characters.
         Which characters are essential to the story? Who fascinates you?
         Which relationships are pivotal?
         How do the characters and key relationships change during the story?

      4. Stageable Image. What is a powerful visual image in the story?
         What would be fun about seeing characters in some of the locations that the story suggests to your imagination?

      5. Storyline. Summarize the main events of the story in two or three sentences.
         What would you call the climax or central event of the story?

      6. Action. Are there events in the story that you can imagine including in your adaptation in physically stageable ways?

D. Imagine a scene for your adaptation based on a favorite scene from your source. Can you picture it playing well onstage? You may want to go ahead and write it out now. How does it read?

E. Of these six building blocks, decide which one, at this stage, has most captured your attention and why.

To someone you trust, state what you find most compelling and back up your claim that this is a powerful aspect of the original story with two examples from the text.

Does articulating this choice challenge your conviction about it? Did your trusted person feel that it was compelling? A story about a broken marriage trying to recover might not be accessible to someone who has never been married. It might be too easy for you, on the other hand, to project yourself onto that story if you are in a troubled relationship. Ideally you want a listener who can offer you perspective, who can relate to the story in a way that your intended audience—most likely a general audience—might.

F. Of the remaining five building blocks, list in descending order of importance to you which are most compelling.

For your two most compelling, reflect on and write down what this aspect of the story makes you think of, drawn from your personal experience of people, events, places, or other works of art. You have intuitive connections to the work already. Find out what they are.

If you have been thinking through this step on your own, now share, with your trusted peer, this further layer of why these other elements intrigue you; talk it through. In this way you challenge yourself to plumb the depths of your emotional and intellectual connection to the story.

If you find yourself with only one or two of the criteria and falter when telling the why to a friend, I'd suggest moving on to a new choice. This discovery would be equivalent to getting worked up over a new relationship and then discovering that you are only interested in your partner's great body or money or Ivy League pedigree; a deeper passion is necessary to make the relationship last.

You should come away from this chapter with a strong notion of why you want to work on this material to start constructing your adaptation. To assure that you have a strong foundation, you should have compelling answers for at least three of the six building blocks we will work through. If what most compels you is thematic (the sociocultural life of Americans in the 1930s, for example, or how parents shape their children), you have a cornerstone on which to build. And it is usually essential that you find either a character or a relationship compelling, as this provides the humanizing connection to the piece. The actual language, in the form of dialogue or evocative prose, adds bedrock from the literary source itself. Once you are sure of the piece you want to adapt, your next step is to create a working template for your adaptation.

2 • *Building Block Two*

Select Dialogue and Narrative

Along with the stage's ability to find unique environments and dramatic structures for telling a story, theater's advantage over literature is its provocative ability to represent multiple points of view with living bodies and live images. Depending on the skill and intention of the writer, a play invites its audience and sometimes forces us into the human arena of deciding who is right or wrong, whose truth we are sympathetic to. The story doesn't reach us from the disembodied ether: actors deliver it to us through their dialogue with other actors, through their storytelling, and through their actions.

What attaches the narrative of your source to the world of a play is a character's specific point of view. In the challenging ensemble plays of Molière, Chekhov, Ibsen, and Miller, we contend with points of view that carry competing weight. The challenge and pleasure of encountering plays by these masters of the craft are in our split sympathies for Sonya, Astrov, and Vanya in *Uncle Vanya* or Willy, Linda, and Biff in *Death of a Salesman,* with each character revealing a unique personal point of view as the story progresses.

Literature is often written in the first person, so the story's narrator is also the principal character. Literature can incisively express a single point of view; often the thrill of reading a skillfully written story is in seeing the world unfold from one character's distinct perspective. The abstemious half of Siamese twin brothers reveals his plight and the peccadilloes of his physically abhorrent, attached front brother in John Barth's "Petition." In theatrical form, you can see the reactions of the actor playing the front brother and allow him sounds or even some of the text in response to the point of view of the complaining back brother. Ishmael guides us in *Moby Dick,* as does the girl in Alice Sebold's *The Lovely Bones,*

Fig. 3. *Black Witness.* The Baldwin character weighs good and evil. (Bob Devin Jones, Theater Emory, 1990.)

Jake Barnes in Hemingway's *The Sun Also Rises,* and Gulliver in Jonathan Swift's *Gulliver's Travels.*

Even in many stories written in the third person, the author chooses to restrict the narration primarily to the viewpoint of one main character by revealing the inner thoughts of that one character and following that character's actions much more closely than any of the others'. Frank Manley approached the story of *The Cockfighter* in this way, rarely leaving the perspective of the boy, who is the story's main character.

Theater's Advantage: Seeing Each Character's Point of View

In adapting any of these first-person stories for the stage as anything but a monologue, you must relinquish the unifying single viewpoint and contend with the complexity of multiple characters judged on their own terms. To bring the story's other characters onstage is to give them their own voices and perspectives, no longer filtered through the perceptions of a first-person narrator. We can and must shift the point of view with each character that speaks. As soon as they open their mouths, we believe that the characters speak for themselves. As in life, we believe each of the speakers—unless we discover a reason to doubt their reliability. The adaptor could establish a certain character as a liar, for instance. Or in sad Ophelia's situation, since her meddlesome father pressures her to deceive her boyfriend Hamlet, we learn to question her sincerity.

In *The Grapes of Wrath,* Steinbeck narrates from the point of view of an omniscient storyteller, as does Tolstoy in *War and Peace,* Edith Wharton in *The Age of Innocence,* and Tom Wolfe in *A Man in Full.* This allows us to see through the eyes or into the mind of any character, describing scenes that have no human witness, such as the details of an empty landscape. Such a narration has the option of maintaining a certain objectivity about the events in the story. But an adaptation for theater filters the story through the subjective points of view of the characters who enact it.

One form of fiction makes a theaterlike choice: writing from multiple points of view, which may prove ripe for adaptation. For examples of this kind of multivoiced writing, see Virginia Woolf's *The Waves,* Penelope Lively's *Moon Tiger,* and Edith Wharton's *The Reef.* In each the narrative perspective shifts from one character to another, taking us inside the thoughts of each in turn. Similarly, onstage we see each character in his or her own light, speaking personal versions of the truth from distinct points of view.

One notable exception is a single-person monologue that can have a secondary point of view, possibly constructed by the playwright and the audience in collusion. For instance, an unreliable narrator-protagonist can unwittingly give herself away by what she says, making the members of the audience active participants in trying to arrive at their own truth. Whether you are adapting from a single point of view or an omniscient one, you must relinquish either in order to give your adaptation the multiple points of view that theater requires. You may choose to follow one main character's thoughts and actions most closely, but you will still need the other characters to have voices of their own. As Joyce Carol Oates explained in an article for the *New York Times,*

> . . . as soon as you begin the task of adaptation, you discover that it isn't "adapting" but "transposing" you must do. The essential dif-

ference between prose fiction and drama is that in prose fiction it is
the narrative voice, the writerly voice, that tells the story; in drama,
of course, characters' voices are usually unmediated, direct. The
prose writer's sheltering cocoon of language dissolves and what
is exposed is the bare skeleton of dialogue, action, subterranean-
subtextual movement. Suddenly, everything must be dramatized
for the eye and the ear; nothing can be summarized. (5)

Creative Partnership:
Reassigning Dialogue to Different Points of View

Adapting literature is a kind of raid. Anthony Minghella, the late adaptor of several novels, including *The English Patient, Cold Mountain,* and
The Talented Mr. Ripley, believed in raiding unapologetically and with
confidence. Minghella said, "It's, in some ways, an argument with the
book—an argument which involves emphasizing what I think is extraordinary, telling the story in the most pungent and powerful way, and
being prepared to make some quite dramatic alterations to the source
material" (Spitz, 76). In his film adaptation of *The English Patient,* we see
the world from subjective points of view, with the eye of the camera taking the viewer to selected aspects of the story.

John Milius and Francis Ford Coppola took a different approach to
point of view in the film *Apocalypse Now,* in which they freely adapted
Joseph Conrad's African-set novella *Heart of Darkness* to an entirely different time and place. The film audience follows the story from the subjective perspective of Captain Willard, played by Martin Sheen, as he gets
closer to his prey, deep in the jungle of Vietnam.

As will be discussed in chapter 3, on character, most adaptations have
one or two principal characters. Unless you are adapting literature with
multiple storylines and subplots, as in a Chekhov play, and intend to
retain them all, you will need to reduce the number of characters by
combining them. This entails reassigning dialogue to your principal
characters, or to a handful of utility characters that play multiple functions in your adaptation. Assigning narrative information to different
characters changes and sometimes broadens the perspective of the original source material. Paradoxically, the creative mandate is to stay true to
the nature of the original text.

Minghella called this creative partnership an argument, one that
can dramatically alter the way the story is told. Compare novelist Marcel

Proust's massive, multivolume *Remembrance of Times Past/In Search of Lost Time* to Harold Pinter's elliptical, elegant, and much shorter screenplay adaptation. Other adaptors, such as the producing/directing team of Merchant and Ivory, focused on adhering as closely as possible to the text and the sequence of scenes in the source material, for example, in *A Room with a View* and *Howards End*.

Whatever their approach, adaptors must stay true to what compelled them to adapt the literature in the first place. And for material not in the public domain, the challenge is to do so within the copyright agreement with the author, within any permission granted to alter the text. In literary adaptations, the inherent complication of making a stageworthy play is in heightening the conflict to sustain the tension while retaining the distinctive verbal style of writers as diverse as Steinbeck, Dickens, Manley, Barth, Soyinka, or Beckett.

Example from The Grapes of Wrath:
Shifting from Omniscient Narration to Multiple Points of View

In one six-page chapter of *The Grapes of Wrath*, when describing the hustle of selling cars to migrant workers, Steinbeck switches the point of view from that of an omniscient storyteller to a car salesman. For his staged version of the novel, Galati adapted that chapter into a single page of script, creating five singing hustlers selling cars.

From the novel:

There's a dumb-bunny looking at that Chrysler. Find out if he got any jack in his jeans. Some of these farm boys is sneaky. Soften 'em up an' roll 'em in to me, Joe. You're doing good. . . .

Square noses, round noses, rusty noses, shovel noses, and the long curve of the streamlines and the flat surfaces before streamlining. Bargains Today. Old monsters with deep upholstery—you can cut her into a truck easy. Two-wheel trailers, axles rusty in the hard afternoon sun. Used Cars. Good Used Cars. Clean, runs good. Don't pump oil . . . Cadillacs, LaSalles, Buicks, Plymouths, Packards, Chevies, Fords, Pontiacs. Row on row, headlights glinting in the afternoon sun. Good Used Cars. (84–85)

Adapted for the stage:

1ST SALESMAN: Used cars.

2ND SALESMAN: Good used cars.

3RD SALESMAN: Cheap transportation.

4TH SALESMAN: Used cars.

ALL FOUR SALESMEN: (singing) Cadillacs, LaSalles, Buicks, Plymouths, Packards, Chevies, Fords, Pontiacs. Soften them up, Joe. Jesus. I wisht I had a thousand jalopies! Get 'em ready to deal an' I'll close 'em. Goin' to California? Here's just what you need. (A rusted heap of truck rolls over the expanse of dust and wood. The front is a Hudson Super Six sedan, its top cut off in the middle and a truck bed fitted on.) She looks shot, but they's thousan's of miles in her. Get 'em ready to deal, an' I'll close 'em.

1ST SALESMAN (speaking): There's a dumb-bunny lookin' at the Graham. See if he has any jack in his jeans.

2ND SALESMAN (speaking): Some of these farm boys is sneaky.

1ST SALESMAN (speaking): Soften 'em up an 'roll 'em in to me, Joe. You're doin' good. (15)

By assigning the lines to different characters, albeit generic salesmen, Galati separates the traits of each somewhat. Salesman 1 reads as predatory, while 2 worries that he may be taken by the "rube." If you read them aloud, you will start to sense their different points of view and distinct strategies. In the adaptation, Galati is able to use the hustlers selling the car to establish the cutaway Hudson Super Six sedan that the Joads buy. And he uses an entertaining musical form, which also softens the harsh edge of the hustle.

Dialogue: The Building Block of Playwrights

Dialogue is talk. You can take it directly from the text and assign it to the characters to speak. Playwrights employ dialogue as their primary tool to reveal story, theme, and conflict through what the characters say, including what they say about what they do, as well as about what others do. Dialogue expresses the characters' needs and the obstacles they face; it reveals how they change over the journey of the play.

Less is often more with dialogue, that is, it is often better to err on the side of fewer words than too many. The task is not to hold up a tape recorder to nature but to selectively find the words that evoke the conflicts driving the characters. Remember that you have the power of subtext: what is implied, whether by what is said or what isn't. And in the actors' craft of creating three-dimensional characters using the dialogue, you have a powerful added vehicle that doesn't exist in your original source: their skill in communicating the story nonverbally, through their acting choices, as well as through the words.

Example of Dialogue Lifted Directly from the Novel

The Cockfighter novel gave me a story and a context. The theme and storyline guided me in choosing what focus to take in adapting it for the stage. Next, dialogue was there to be taken in part or often as a whole and transplanted onto the stage in a fertile context.

The central event of the adaptation is the climactic scene, during which Sonny puts the final piece of the puzzle of his identity together while overhearing an argument between his parents. Written almost entirely in dialogue in the novel, the following scene encompassed such great language—and the book's central event, when the father cuts the son loose—that it formed the basis for my adaptation.

MOTHER: Tell me about it.
FATHER: Nothing to tell.
MOTHER: What happened then?
FATHER: Little shit blew it.
MOTHER: It wasn't his fault.
FATHER: The hell it wasn't. Whose fault was it?
MOTHER: He was too young.
FATHER: You mean it's my fault.
MOTHER: I didn't say that. I'm not talking about fault.
FATHER: I am.
MOTHER: I told you. He's just a boy. You shouldn't have trusted him.
FATHER: I didn't trust him. I didn't trust him any more than I trusted that brother of yours.
MOTHER: He had a hard time.
FATHER: Don't give me that, Lily. I had a hard time. You had a hard time. We all had a hard time.
MOTHER: I'm thinking about Sonny.
FATHER: He's all right. He's just a boy.

MOTHER: That's what I mean.

FATHER: That's right. I thought it was time to start him on cocks, but I was wrong. He's too young for it.

MOTHER: You put too big a burden on him. He wasn't ready.

FATHER: Damn right he wasn't ready. He just threw that cock away.

MOTHER: I don't see how he could have known.

FATHER: I'd have known. If it was me, I would have told.

MOTHER: That's silly, Jake. You don't know what you'd do if you were him.

FATHER: I'd have taken an interest in it. You know me. I'd do it like I do right now. I always have, and I always will.

MOTHER: I know that, Jake.

FATHER: I'm not like him. Never have been and never will be. (Shift.)

BOY: As soon as he said that, I knew what it was. The last piece snapped into place. I wasn't him and never would be, and not only that, I never would want to. Each one was different. That was the puzzle. (149–51)

When other drafts of a work exist, the adaptor has the exciting and exacting opportunity to meld them into a theatrical version that serves his or her vision. Many theater artists enjoy this kind of work when assembling a script for a Shakespeare production from the various quartos that exist: the adaptors add lines, assign lines to different characters, or alter the structure.

Lifting this dynamic, complex scene, written in dialogue form, gave me the basis for the adaptation. As the central event of the story, the culminating scene of the fight to make the boy like his mother or his father gave me the boy's recognition. In writing the rest of the adaptation, I had this scene to build toward.

Example of Dialogue Edited for Adapting from The Grapes of Wrath

Here is a pivotal scene from the novel *The Grapes of Wrath:*

"Tom," she whispered, "What's the matter?"

"Sh!" he said. "Don't talk loud. I got in a fight."

"Tom!"

"I couldn' help it, Ma."

She knelt down beside him. "You in trouble?"

He was a long time answering. "Yeah," he said. "In trouble. I can't go out to work. I got to hide."

The children crawled near on their hands and knees, staring greedily. "What's the matter'th him, Ma?"

"Hush!" Ma said. "Go wash up."

"We got no soap."

"Well, use water."

"What's the matter'th Tom?"

"Now you hush. An' don't you tell nobody."

They backed away and squatted down against the far wall, knowing they would not be inspected.

Ma asked, "Is it bad?"

"Nose busted."

"I mean the trouble?"

"Yeah. Bad!"

Al opened his eyes and looked at Tom. "Well, for Chris' sake! What was you in?"

"What's a matter?" Uncle Jon asked.

Pa clumped in. "They was open all right." He put a tiny bag of flour and his package of lard on the floor beside the stove. "'S'a matter?" he asked.

Tom braced himself on one elbow for a moment, and then he lay back. "Jesus, I'm weak. I'm gonna tell ya once. So I'll tell all of ya. How 'bout the kids?"

Ma looked at them, huddled against the wall. "Go wash ya face."

"No," Tom said. "They got to hear. They got to know. They might blab if they don' know."

"What the hell is this?" Pa demanded.

"I'm a-gonna tell. Las' night I went out to see what all the yellin' was about. An' I come on Casy."

"The preacher?"

"Yeah, Pa. The preacher, on'y he was a-leadin' the strike. They come for him."

Pa demanded, "Who come for him?"

"I dunno. Same kinda guys that turned us back on the road that night. Had pick handles." He paused. "They killed 'im. Busted his head. I was standin' there. I went nuts. Grabbed the pick handle." He looked bleakly back at the night, the darkness, the flashlights, as he spoke. "I—I clubbed a guy." (499–500)

In the following excerpt from the play, Galati's galvanizing edit of this scene keeps the focus on the emotional core of the family: Tom and Ma Joad. The adaptation dramatically condenses thirty-eight pages of the novel down to two pages in the script, subtracting the other significant family members, including Pa Joad, Uncle John, Al, and the children. Here is a section of the adapted scene:

MA: Tom, what's the matter?

TOM: Sh! Don't talk loud. I got in a fight. (He stumbles closer to Ma.)

MA: Tom!

TOM: I couldn' help it, Ma.

MA: You in trouble?

TOM: Yeah. In trouble. I can't go out to work. I got to hide. (Tom sits on the bench.)

MA: Is it bad?

TOM: Nose busted.

MA: I mean the trouble.

TOM: Yeah, bad! I went out to see what all the yellin' was about. An' I come on Casy.

MA: The preacher?

TOM: Yeah. The preacher, on'y he was a-leadin' the strike. They come for him.

MA: Who come for him?

TOM: I dunno. Had pick handles. They killed 'im. Busted his head. I was standin' there. I went nuts. Grabbed the pick handle. I—I clubbed a guy. (77)

Tom's famous epiphany about how we are all connected doesn't arrive until page 537 of the novel, well after he shows up battered on page 499. Retaining Tom's bloody condition and his fresh witnessing of the henchmen killing Casy, Galati takes us incisively to the connection of ex-preacher Casy's belief that a better world is possible in the words Tom finds himself gushing to his mother:

TOM: Well, maybe like Casy says, a fella ain't got a soul of his own, but on'y a piece of a big one—an' then—

MA: Then what, Tom?

TOM: Then it don' matter. Then I'll be all aroun' in the dark. I'll be ever'where—wherever you look. Wherever they's a fight so hungry people can eat, I'll be there. Wherever they's a cop beatin' up a guy,

I'll be there. An' when our folks eat the stuff they raise an' live in the houses they build—why, I'll be there. See? God, I'm talkin' like Casy. (78)

Galati included this passage from the novel to turn the scene into the central event for the character of Tom. Here is the passage in the original, from which he adapted it:

Then it don' matter. Then I'll be all aroun' in the dark. I'll be ever'where—wherever you look. Wherever they's a fight so hungry people can eat, I'll be there. Wherever they's a cop beatin' up a guy, I'll be there. If Casy knowed, why, I'll be in the way guys yell when they're mad an'—I'll be in the way kids laugh when they're hungry an' they know supper's ready. An' when our folks eat the stuff they raise an' live in the houses they build—why, I'll be there. See? God, I'm talkin' like Casy. Comes of thinkin' about him so much. Seems like I can see him sometimes. (537)

Example of Dialogue from the Novel, Edited for the Script

Some passages of dialogue in the original text of *The Cockfighter* have rich language that you may want to retain for your script, but they might not play effectively onstage. Unaltered, they would load your scene with too much talk, explanation, description, or repetition. Careful trimming to focus on key language can turn these passages into stageworthy scenes.

Just before the following scene, Sonny's father has found the boy petting their prize cock, which he has named Lion. The father's irritated reaction is to give Sonny a lesson in objectifying the animal, and the father co-opts the wife into helping him teach it to the boy until a bewildered Sonny answers correctly.

They're not pets, he told the boy. You want pets, get your mother to buy one at Easter and raise it by hand. These are wild animals.

What do you call a deer, he said, you see it running in the woods, lifting its scut?

It was the first lesson his daddy ever taught him, and he looked at him, not knowing what to say.

Say Deer, his momma said.

And he said Deer, just like a child, repeating it after her.

And his daddy said, The little shit. Listen to that little son of a bitch, Lily. And he ruffled the boy's hair the same way the boy had seen him ruffle the head of a rooster.

Say it again, you little shit.

The boy said Deer, just like he taught him.

And his daddy said, Damn right! And these are cocks. Remember that. Deer and bear don't have names, and these don't either, except what God gave them, and that's enough. You call them cocks.

The boy said, Yes, sir. (13)

In the play, the actor who plays Sonny can experience and communicate the emotional spin of feeling like a young man at one moment and being under pressure as a child the next. In the adapted script, the edited version reads:

FATHER: They're not pets. You want pets, get your momma to buy one at Easter and raise it by hand. These are wild animals. What you call a deer, you see it running in the woods, lifting its scut?

MOTHER: Tell him deer.

BOY: Deer.

FATHER: The little shit. Listen to that little son of a bitch, Lily. Say deer, you little shit.

BOY: Deer.

FATHER: Damn right. And these are cocks. Remember that. Deers and bears don't have names, and these don't either, except what God gave them, and that's enough. You call them cocks. (120)

The young actor playing the boy can glean clues to the acting of this scene by referring to the cut narration from the novel, a bonus of working on an adaptation, for savvy actors who research their roles. In the novel we learn that the first lesson his daddy ever taught him is here in this scene. An important action that the actors played to reveal some of the father/son relationship was precisely how Dad ruffled the boy's hair, the same way the boy had seen his daddy do it to the prized rooster.

To know where to assign dialogue for my adaptation, I had to know who my main characters were. Questions of text and character work closely together, so your decisions will intertwine, and each will drive choices in the other. Negotiating between the needs of these two building blocks, I arrived at the choice to adapt it for only three actors, with one actress doubling as both the mother and her brother Homer. Then I set about the task of identifying which parts of the material, originally told primarily from Sonny's point of view in the novel, would be best reassigned to the other characters: the mother, the father, or the uncle. The narrative monologues of Lily and Homer, which I quote in full in chapter 3, on character, reveal some of the resulting choices I made.

Narrative: Pacing Your Build

Narrative is storytelling, including summary or descriptive passages, without dialogue. As we attend to the key elements of a play—theme, character, storyline, image—we construct the script primarily through dialogue and action. We usually limit narration, summary, and description to the form of exposition exemplified by the Greek chorus, or to a narrative monologue describing an unstageable event such as an off-stage battle, a coronation, or saving Caesar from drowning in the Tiber River. Adaptations that rely on exquisitely written speeches lifted from the original source may prove that what is eloquent as literature on the page, where the reader can savor it at his or her own pace, often deflates into self-conscious speechifying onstage. An audience member often can't keep up with rich, undramatized text spoken live or, occasionally, if it's dramatically viable but delivered by an underpowered actor.

The language-rich plays of Shakespeare, the Greeks, Chekhov, and contemporary playwrights such as Sam Shepard, Suzan-Lori Parks, and Tony Kushner require that we pay attention to what is said. Often these plays don't translate well to film, a more visual medium, unless the film successfully balances all those words with physical action and imagery, not just scenes of people talking. The playwright's ability to keep language in the balance calls for involving the audience in the character's story.

Language drives literary adaptation, by its very nature. And the skill to cull both evocative narrative and workable dialogue from the text is the great challenge of the adaptor.

We get caught up in the narrative drive of a novel, knowing that we can pause to refresh our perspective whenever we need to. We can reread the paragraph or chapters, ruminate on a line or image, or put the book down to discuss why the character is acting this way. But we rarely need the pause button as we watch a DVD at home because the medium of film, like theater, operates in compressed time, where the excitement of viewing is in the knowledge that the story will unfold before us within the two-hour traffic of performance.

Still, if we're watching a film at home and the story is confusing, then the pause button and a little rewind might retrieve the lost connection. Theater, with its uniqueness in being live and never able to repeat exactly what you just witnessed, can't give you that option. As we adapt from one medium to another, we must keep that unique playwriting pleasure and challenge in mind.

How to Handle Different Kinds of Narration

Narration, summary, and description are writing tools used to investigate a story. In fiction the narrator usually tells the story in the past tense. The narrator's rhythm in describing details pulls us into a slow, meditative state, like watching words paint the story. Summary, in contrast, accelerates—more like snapshots. These modes of perception are a challenge in the theater, where we want the action to be in the present as often as possible. We want the characters, and ourselves along with them, hurtling forward to an unknown future. Generally theater excels at portraying the social, external world, while fiction takes us inside ourselves, more to the psychological and personal world.

The Royal Shakespeare Company's two-evening, nine-hour *Nicholas Nickleby,* adapted by David Edgar from the Dickens novel, felt somewhat weighed down with too much narrative exposition early in the play, but it shed this weight and became increasingly dynamic as it moved forward. Thus, paradoxically, it felt shorter the longer it went on. The gifted playwright David Edgar adapted *Nickleby* in collaboration with members of the RSC, and they apparently considered the exposition crucial to establishing the six building blocks, particularly to setting up prior circumstances, such as I discuss in chapter 5, on storyline. Establishing prior circumstance (the technique of seeding what happened before the story we are watching began) is brilliantly controlled by Henrik Ibsen in his plays *Ghosts* and *The Master Builder.* Making past dramatic actions viably present is delicate business. Often clunky, obvious information is put into the mouths of poorly defined characters instead of being dramatized. Remember Basil Exposition from the *Austin Powers* movies?

You will discover that your most viable technique for presenting narrative is channeling it through an active character engaged in the main conflict. A vital character's laying out of crucial information, as Prospero does to his trapped, ignorant, innocent daughter Miranda at the beginning of *The Tempest,* plays dramatically.

Even though most literature adapted for the stage was originally constructed to include both narrative and dialogue, some plays can come from purely narrative sources, written without dialogue, such as Samuel Beckett's "Enough" and John Barth's "Petition." Adapting a completely narrative story to the stage, you may keep it intact as a monologue or divide the material by assigning it to multiple characters, as was done in one admired production of the late Sarah Kane's fragmentary drama *4.48 Psychosis.* In adapting the novel or short story for the stage, one occasionally has the happy option of taking it as a whole and uncut, or nearly so—only slightly edited and rearranged—to stage it in its entirety. Beckett's "Enough," told from the point of view of a woman leaving her husband, and Barth's "Petition" (retitled *Me and My Shadow* for the stage), in which the point of view is Eng's, the back brother of a pair of Siamese twins, are examples of entire narratives that could be lifted to the stage. I share the details of how in chapter 7 (see the section "Two Case Studies").

There are several techniques for transforming narrative into dialogue. As you get to know your material, look for ways to apply one of the following approaches.

Example from The Cockfighter:
Narration Assigned to Help Define the Characters

Short, verbatim sections of narrative from the novel *The Cockfighter* show up in the theatrical adaptation. What translates the style of narration into the present tense of theatrical time is the focus on a character's point of view. At the beginning of the novel, there is an epigraph from the German Christian mystic and theologian Jacob Boehme: "The Spirit of Man is descended not only from the Stars and the Elements, but there is hid therein a Spark of the Light and the Power of God." Then the novel begins with this narration:

> The boy waited until the moon rose and the aluminum frame of the window beside him was full of cold light. He watched it as it crept up on the bed and when it finally got to the slash of electrified red that ran up the middle of the quilt his mother made, defining him, he got up and crept down the hall. (9)

In the published script, I assigned the thought and voice of the quotation and opening paragraph to three different characters:

MOTHER AND FATHER: (in silhouette) "The spirit of Man is descended
   not only from the Stars and the Elements, but there is hid therein—"
BOY: (as light reveals him) "a Spark of the Light and Power of God."
(Shift. We see the boy rise.)
FATHER: The boy waited until the moon rose and the aluminum frame of
   the window beside him was full of cold light. He watched as it crept
   up on the bed, and when it finally got to the slash of electrified red
   that ran up the middle of the quilt his mother made, defining him,
   he got up and crept down the hall. (119)

This distribution establishes a family steeped in a religious culture. The boy speaks the last part of the quotation, as he represents the Inner Light imagery throughout the story. Following the primordial feel of the family bloodline, the adaptation seizes on the inherent religious values and Inner Light imagery of Boehme's passage to establish a ritual world of family. I assigned the opening narration of the novel to the voice and point of view of the father. The novelist's narrative technique is to employ the voice of an omniscient, much older Sonny, looking back on his transition into adulthood. He tells the story of facing becoming like either his mother or his father or finding his own way. In fracturing this narrative style into multiple points of view for the stage, the adaptor gains several layers of perception. The father's opening descriptive narration establishes the "cold light" and stealthy action of a boy creeping through the dark, assured world of the father.

A strategy in this adaptation was to follow the novel's lead and hear the story the way the boy is directly experiencing it, or how he would remember it, thus keeping him from the omniscient view. If this scene painting were assigned to the son, he would become too knowledgeable, too present to his own predicament.

The stage: a cockpit with wire-framed cages for furniture pieces was bathed in cool blue light with the parents asleep on the ground, the only source of warm light coming from the empty cage that Sonny is creeping toward to find the hidden spark of light. This simple, imaginative environment, guided by lighting and differentiated voices, helped the audience take in the slower descriptive narrative of the novel. The staging also helped bring the narrative into the more present-tense timeline of live theater.

Example from The Cockfighter:
A Narrative Selection Used as a Monologue

Another way to adapt a narrative passage from your source is to assign it all to one character as a monologue, which may or may not need to be edited down from the original.

In *The Cockfighter*, the action after the opening sequence reverts to a longer wake-up scene, which culminates in the father's telling the mother that he will teach the boy to shoot a gun. This prompts the boy's first narrative monologue, which I edited from the third-person narration of the novel into the first-person of the boy speaking.

> BOY: I couldn't believe it. I never even thought about wanting a gun, but now that my daddy mentioned it and my momma didn't seem to mind, that's all I wanted. I already had me a cock. All I needed now was a gun. Growing up is the most exciting thing that ever happened to me. Every day it's something new. Today me and Lion. Next week a gun. (124)

The inner soliloquy voice of Sonny is more articulate than a not quite thirteen year old's would be, waking up and hearing an argument through his thin bedroom wall. In the best literary adaptations, such a difference creates a dramatic tension between what the character is experiencing in the present and what a reflective voice would remember in looking back on climactic moments of the past.

Example from The Grapes of Wrath:
Dramatic Compression of Narrative-Based Dialogue

In one sequence, Galati compresses dialogue and narrative into a character he aptly names "Man Going Back," who warns the Joads of the impending disappointment and troubles the journey will bring them:

> MAN GOING BACK: Me—I'm comin' back. I been there. I'm goin' to starve. I'd ruther starve all over at once.
> PA: What the hell you talkin' about? I got a han'bill says they got good wages, an' little while ago I seen a thing in the paper says they need folks to pick fruit.
> MAN GOING BACK: I don' wanna fret you.

TOM: You ain't gonna fret us. You done some jackassin'. You ain't gonna shut up now. The han'bill says they need men.

MAN GOING BACK: You don't know what kind a men they need.

TOM: What you talkin' about?

MAN GOING BACK: Look. How many men they say they want on your han'bill?

PA: Eight hunderd, an' that's in one little place.

MAN GOING BACK: Orange color han'bill?

PA: Why—yes.

MAN GOING BACK: Give the name a the fella—says so and so, labor contractor? (Pa reaches in his pocket and brings out a folded orange handbill.)

PA: That's right. How'd you know?

MAN GOING BACK: Look. It don't make no sense. The fella wants eight hunderd men. So he prints up five thousand of them things an' maybe twenty thousan' people sees 'em. An' maybe two-three thousan' folks get movin' on account of this here han'bill. Folks that's crazy with worry.

PA: But it don't make no sense!

MAN GOING BACK: Not till you see the fella that put on this here bill. You'll see him, or somebody that's working for him. You'll be a-campin' by a ditch, you an' fifty other families. An' he'll look in your tent an' see if you got anything lef' to eat. An' if you got nothin', he says, "Wanna job?" An' you'll say, "I sure do, mister. I'll sure thank you for a chance to do some work." An' he'll say, "I can use you." An' you'll say, "When do I start?" An' he'll tell you where to go, an' what time, an' then he'll go on. Maybe he needs two hunderd men, so he talks to five hunderd, an' they tell other folks an' when you get to the place, they's a thousan' men. This here fella says, "I'm payin' twenty cents an hour." An' maybe half the men walk off. But they's still five hunderd that's so goddamn hungry they'll work for nothin' but biscuits. (35–36)

Now notice in the excerpt from *The Grapes of Wrath* novel by Steinbeck what Galati chose from to create the scene in the adaptation:

The ragged man said slowly, "Me—I'm comin' back. I been there."

The faces turned quickly toward him. The men were rigid. The hiss of the lantern dropped to a sigh and the proprietor lowered the front chair legs to the porch, stood up, and pumped the lantern until the hiss was sharp and high again. He went back to his chair, but he did not tilt back again. The ragged man turned toward the faces. "I'm goin' back to starve. I ruther starve all over at oncet."

Pa said, "What the hell you talkin' about? I got a han'bill says they got good wages, an' little while ago I seen a thing in the paper says they need folks to pick fruit."

The ragged man turned to Pa. "You got any place to go, back home?"

"No," said Pa. "We're out. They put a tractor past the house."

"You wouldn' go back then?"

"'Course not."

"Then I ain't gonna fret you," said the ragged man.

"'Course you ain't gonna fret me. I got a han'bill says they need men. Don't make no sense if they don't need men. Costs money for them bills. They wouldn' put 'em out if they didn' need men."

"I don' wanna fret you."

Pa said angrily, "You done some jackassin'. You ain't gonna shut up now. My han'bill says they need men. You laugh an' say they don't. Now, which one's a liar?"

The ragged man looked down into Pa's angry eyes. He looked sorry. "Han'bill's right," he said. "They need men."

"Then why the hell you stirrin' us up laughin'?"

"'Cause you don't know what kind of men they need."

"What you talkin' about?"

The ragged man reached a decision. "Look," he said. "How many men they say they want on your han'bill?"

"Eight hunderd, an' that's in one little place."

"Orange color han'bill?"

"Why—yes."

"Give the name a the fella—says so and so, labor contractor?"

Pa reached in his pocket and brought out the folded handbill. "That's right. How'd you know?"

"Look," said the man. "It don't make no sense. This fella wants eight hunderd men. So he prints up five thousand of them things an' maybe twenty thousan' people sees 'em. An' maybe two-three thousan' folks get movin' on account a this here han'bill. Folks that's crazy with worry."

"But it don't make no sense!" Pa cried.

"Not till you see the fella that put out this here bill. You'll see him, or somebody that's workin' for him. You'll be a-campin' by a ditch, you an' fifty other families. An' he'll look in your tent an' see if you got anything lef' to eat. An' if you got nothin', he says, 'Wanna job?' An' you'll say, 'I sure do, mister. I'll sure thank you for a chance to do some work.' An' he'll say, 'I can use you.' An' you'll say, 'When do I start?' An' he'll tell you where to go, an' what time, an' then he'll go on. Maybe he needs two hunderd men, so he talks to five hunderd, an' they tell other folks an' when you get to the place, they's a thousan' men. This here fella says, 'I'm payin' twenty cents an hour.' An' maybe half the men walk off. But they's still five hunderd that's so goddamn hungry they'll work for nothin' but biscuits." (243–44)

Galati took the man's expository dialogue mostly as is and in its chronological order. He did move Pa's "you ain't gonna fret me" to follow the Man Going Back's later "I don't want to fret you." This move tightens the exchange, allowing us to experience the fretful situation as the actors let us in on the conflict through acting, rather than through the words that repeat how fretful they feel.

Also notice the descriptive material around the dialogue in the original. Immediately after the man's first line, Steinbeck writes, "The faces turned quickly toward him. The men were rigid." Both images are evocative clues to staging the scene. You may want to include some key part of these actions in the stage directions for your script, and certainly your director and actors may find these descriptions useful as they research the characters.

Example from The Cockfighter *of Summary*
Exposition Played Dramatically

In the climactic cockfight of *The Cockfighter,* Sonny's gambling father sets him up to fight the champion cock that he gave his son as a gift. As in the opening scene, when Sonny creeps out to hold this pet that he secretly calls Lion, the emotional attachment continues to grow between the boy and the animal. Believing that the audience's imagination would create a reality for an imagined Lion better than a real chicken, a stuffed one, or a creative prop, I bet on their emotional identification with the struggle of a father to make his son become like him in the face of the boy's rebellion to become himself. I chose to allow the summary narrative of the final cockfight to be a vocal duel in the relationship between father and mother over the son, with neither a real nor a made-to-look-like cockfight.

> MOTHER AND FATHER: Ok, you ready? Ok, bill them up. Pit them! The cocks flew at one another like they were fired out of a barrel. They hit and went rolling over and over on top of each other. It was hard to tell where one left off and the other started. They looked like some kind of ball of fire or wheel of feathers, kicking up dust. Then they hit the wire, and it knocked them apart, and they ran at one another again and got hung up with the gaffs in each other so deep they couldn't move. They just lay there on top of each other kicking their feet as though they were wired, trying to get up. (141)

The two actors voiced the language almost simultaneously, leading each other on through the words. The father played the text brutal and fast, the mother aghast and recoiling. Sonny, deeply empathetic with his pet, physicalized the fight in his body—each gash a received wound that asked the audience to identify further with the boy's learned violence and eventual atrocity. While the language is rich and evocative and the actors did all they could to vocalize the fight, the experience for the audience was mixed, in that their expectation was for a high-noon fight, which instead they had to imagine. And while the novel's author, on seeing the stage adaptation, was partly frustrated by the lack of a realistic fight that would have made tangible the demise of Lion, keeping the focus on what was happening to the boy was dramatically successful in terms of character and storyline.

Balancing necessary narration with dramatic action driven by relationships and conflict is pivotal to a successful adaptation. What makes narration work is the degree to which the audience hears the narrative not only as commentary but also as a revelation of the characters' inner lives. The narrative passages invite the audience to share private feelings, observations, and conflicts that few or none of the other characters know about. Such narrative passages allow you to include material from the omniscient authorial voice of your source, played from a specific character's point of view. The skillful adaptor tends to privilege dialogue from the original over narrative passages, preserving dialogue even if it needs to be assigned to other characters. And the narrative is pruned so as not

to overwhelm the audience with too much information. *The Cockfighter,*
Nicholas Nickleby, and *The Grapes of Wrath* are examples of this more usual
approach of significantly editing the text.

Example from The Grapes of Wrath: *Adapting Narration into Action*

Late in Galati's play version of *The Grapes Of Wrath,* he accomplishes
a remarkable sequence of dramatic compression. He layers together
scenes separated by almost one hundred pages of text in the original,
and the entire dramatic sequence is telescoped into two pages of script.
In four pools of light Galati establishes

- The Joad son Al courting his girl
- Rose touching her earlobes, remembering the gold earrings Ma had
  given her for her newly pierced ears
- Tom and Ma dancing in the weed patch camp dance
- A "Lean Man" stepping into a pool of light and narrating, "The moving, questing people were migrants now. Those families which had
  lived on a little piece of land, who had lived and died on forty acres,
  had now the whole west to rove." (69–70)

Galati is able to stage the wider world into which the Joads are thrown.
The generations of the Joad family are becoming further scattered as
they encounter the new conflicts and possibilities on their journey.

Research on Language

Although some writers adopt varying styles when writing about different places, classes, and times, most sustain a signature style. There is a
consistency in the language, characters, and locations in the works of
Samuel Beckett, J. M. Coetzee, Jorge Luis Borges, Alice Walker, or Margaret Atwood. One way to hear the cadences of a writer's language style
and construction is to compare them to the author's other writings.

When I compared Frank Manley's other novels, plays, and short stories, an identifiable language style emerged: blunt, dialect-inflected syntax using everyday words. These other examples helped me to see more
vividly what was specific to the character evocations in the language in
The Cockfighter. For me to edit dialogue for a character as unique as Jake

(the father), or to assign narration to him in order to hear it from his point of view, it was imperative that I pay close attention to Jake's rhythm, word choices, and length of delivery. We tune our playwriting ear for clarity of character by listening for specific words, phrases, and idioms that distinguish a father from a son, a mother from an uncle. Trying to capture the musicality that we've also heard in the narrating voice of the original work, we should be careful to assign new points of view in ways that add variety and nuance to the characters.

Here are excerpts from two of Manley's other published writings. The first is from *The Evidence,* his first play written directly for the stage:

GEORGE: He was sleeping under the tarp. I was sitting down by the fire, trying to get my feet warm. My socks were smoking. Steam was coming out of the toes. I just put on a piece of wet wood. It was sizzling against the dark of the trees like a thin fog when all of a sudden I heard something. I looked up.

LEE: And that's when he saw it.

GEORGE: It crept up to the fire and looked at me through the smoke.

(14)

The second is from the short story "The Rain of Terror," which Manley later adapted into a play that starred Kathy Bates at the Humana Festival of New American Plays:

"My name is Oletta Crews."

It sounded like a public announcement.

"This is James Terry Crews, my husband." She indicated the old man on the sofa beside her. He was dressed in khaki trousers and six-inch work boots. The woman had on a print dress, a bold floral pattern like slashes. She wore no shoes.

James Terry Crews gestured silently, acknowledging himself.

"Don't act like an idiot," Oletta Crews said, and the man dropped his hand.

"Just sit there." She turned away from him.

"This is James Terry Crews, my husband." She spoke in a powerful voice, lifted like a singer's from her diaphragm. "He's retired. We're both retired," she added significantly. "Him from work and me from housework. I got a bad heart, and I'm stout besides. You can see that. Doctor says I'm hundreds of pounds overweight, shortening my life with every bite of food I take. But what if I didn't? You think that'd help?" She leaned forward and spoke confidently. "There's more dies of hunger than does of the other." (24–25)

Both selections attest to Manley's acclaimed gift for observing the southern, rural, working-class speech and lifestyle. As much as I might have wanted to truncate the speech for simplicity and time, or correct its grammar for comprehension, I ultimately found that the character's language, spoken by a good actor, revealed them.

✦ ✦ ✦ ✦

CONSTRUCTION EXERCISES FOR BUILDING BLOCK 2

A. Having reread your source three times while finalizing your choice of material, you're now ready to read it in search of its most adaptable passages. Use two different colored highlighters, one for narrative and one for dialogue, if it exists. Highlight the text that is most evocative to you or best tells the story. At this stage let go of trying to make corrections or force a structure.
   - From your highlighted sections, cut and paste, in chronological order, the narrative and dialogue sections that you found most compelling.
   - Read those sections sequentially.
   - Read them again, this time noting which storyline is evoked in the cut-and-paste version.
   - Notice which one or two characters' points of view are emerging as primary. Whose voice do you hear most often?
   - Note what is gained and what is lost in moving from the original source to your reconstructed version.

   Now you have a frame in which to work as you learn about the rest of the building blocks that will shape your adaptation. As you make choices about character, storyline, and image—choices that continue to build on your focal theme—you will find passages that need to be added and some that need to be eliminated as you move forward from this initial cut-and-paste draft. And the material in this first pass will also feed your choices about what's important in each of those building blocks.

B. To measure the strength and weight of your adaptation at this initial chronological cut-and-paste stage, have friends (or, better yet, actors) read the version to you. Your only task is to listen, pen and paper in hand,

and take notes. What still feels compelling to you? What feels repetitive or too hard to follow? At the end of the reading, ask your readers what they found compelling and what story emerged for them. Note these reactions as a possible guide to what material to cut, rearrange, or add from the source material.

C. Choose a favorite dialogue-based scene and write a fresh draft of it. Decide whether you need to edit, summarize, or reorder it based on what you've learned from the examples in this chapter. Pay attention to the dramatic point of the scene.

D. Find a narrative-based scene that gives information that is crucial to your story. Make a choice about which character could best deliver this information in your play and adapt it for your script. Remember some of the possibilities that you've learned in this chapter about how to make narrative playable.

Reading your template version of dialogue and narration will reveal your success so far in finding the story. In my adaptation of *The Cockfighter*, my cut and paste revealed that my focus was on three primary characters, and this knowledge allowed me to let go of a dozen others. The story was mostly about the bloodline struggle of the mom and dad to shape the son.

For each of the coming chapters on essential building blocks, you will be writing or rewriting scenes. When you do, refer as needed to the examples in this chapter of how to adapt dialogue and narrative to remind yourself of possibilities for ways to use them. Now that you have the template of a first cut-and-paste draft, the rest of the process of building your adaptation will be about improving and changing it, however radically you need to, in order to make it work. You'll be honing specific scenes and adding and cutting as you get clearer about what is working and what is not. Your adaptation is taking shape.

3 • *Building Block Three*

Identify Principal Characters and Primary Relationships

Characters have confided their secrets and revealed their contradictions to their original author. As adaptors, we must share the hidden diary of their motivations, making our own choices about what to reveal about the characters and how by selecting actions and dialogue that illuminate them. Theater, the most forensic art, sets up that challenge.

Personality is impossible to define. It includes an unlimited array of personal tastes, habits, and ways of being. Created at the crossroads of nature and nurture—genetics, environment, and experience—personality exists in the vast temporal expanse of past, present, and future; it changes over time, loses certain threads for a while, and picks them back up years later. We may approach some understanding of our own personality, but we can never fully understand another person's, not even a fictional character's, because there will always be those ineffable, inexplicable moments that make them uniquely who they are.

Character, however, can be defined. It is a discernible array of traits fixed by place, time, gender, class, and psychology. Character is like a photo album of a specific time in a person's life. For a play it's the time encompassed by its storyline. A character for theater exists in specific places, in particular relationships, wearing selected pieces of clothing, and with distinctive traits. Character is a lens that focuses on selected aspects of personality and allows us to comprehend a person's actions.

Short stories and novels describe character. Theater is the genre for revealing characters in action, by what they say and do. The script uncovers their past, conflicts, and relationships by showing them in action. Richly dimensional characters like King Lear, Ma Joad, Uncle Vanya, Linda Loman, and Sonny can exist on the stage in their realizable potential, all idiosyncrasies and contradictions intact, if we allow the adaptation to incorporate what an actor can bring to the role that compliments the author's portrait of the character.

We construct three-dimensional characters first from materials in the novel: what is said by or about the character regarding his or her nature? These facts, which at times are actually lies or self-deception, create the skeletal outline of a character. How the author or other characters describe one another gives you sculpting material to see a character's class, ethnicity, and job. What they do (their actions) gives us their heart and soul. Do they betray someone, whisper when excited, laugh when nervous, hit back when taunted, or avoid looking at someone? These are actions, the things they do that reveal who they are and what is playable for an actor portraying them.

Choosing Which Characters Your Adaptation Will Enact

Most adaptations will have one or two principal characters and one or two primary relationships. From the work you did in choosing your material, you already have some sense of who the main characters are likely to be in your adaptation. This chapter will help you to solidify that choice.

Choosing which character is primary and which details you want to reveal about that character is your divine right as an adaptor. Even if you want the entire novel played or read onstage, how you conceive the characters and what you choose to emphasize reflect your interpretation of the work. In *Rosencrantz and Guildenstern Are Dead,* Tom Stoppard adapted *Hamlet* to tell the story of Hamlet's hapless college buddies. While in this version Hamlet is way upstage somewhere, figuring out how to be, Rosencrantz and Guildenstern are center stage, grinding through the political machine of Denmark. There are also adaptations of *Hamlet* that focus on the Gertrude-Ophelia relationship. And while Tom Joad is the principal character in both Steinbeck's and Galati's *Grapes of Wrath,* an adaptor could do a powerful feminist take on the story by making Ma Joad the central character and concentrating on her relationship with her daughter Rose. Consider which characters can and should be primary and which secondary in your adaptation.

Primary characters are the ones whose journey we follow through the play. It's their story. The arc of their adventure—what they discover, what obstacles thwart their desires, who they relate to or not—is what compels us to follow the story. Often there is a protagonist (a sympathetic character essential to the story) and an antagonist (who opposes the protagonist and what he or she seeks). Secondary characters can be less well developed; they will be spending a lot less time on stage and may even be double cast with other parts. You can recognize likely secondary characters when your response to them while reading the original material isn't as strong, and when they don't catch your interest as much as the characters who will be primary in your adaptation. Usually the primary characters in the original will also be primary in your script, but not necessarily. Consider Horton Foote's experience:

> But there are times, for instance, when I was dramatizing Faulkner's story, "Tomorrow," the character of the woman became alive to me even though Faulkner gives only a few paragraphs to her. He told me enough about her so that my imagination began to work, and she became somebody I knew. (11)

Trust your own instincts about which characters are the right ones to tell your particular version of this story.

Know Your Characters Intimately

Adaptors have the power and authority of Prospero: they can make characters come alive, disappear, merge into one another—and change sex, shape, age, or even their destiny. Building great characters requires knowing each one's strategy for living, for staying alive. Is being secure most vital to their sense of themselves? Is it a happy family, fame, adventure, danger, honesty, sex, or power? It is crucial to define one drive that keeps them enticingly alive, so that you can draw your principal character vividly for the stage.

Konstantin Stanislavski's system of playable objectives and intentions is the method actors most often use. Having some knowledge of this technique and of the actor's process is useful to the adaptor, in order to understand what is actable onstage.

Objectives and intentions involve defining what characters want and what they would do to get it. If Gertrude wants Hamlet to calm down, she might speak soothingly to him and stroke his neck. Don't use text that only sounds good, no matter how poetic. As the adaptor, it is crucial that you find words that lead to playable actions. Your job is to translate your reading imagination into the three-dimensional reality of characters who talk in order to influence others (or yell, cajole, surprise). You can feed the actors' work by including the moments when characters mush a grapefruit in a face, back away in fear, or hold someone tenderly.

A well-defined character will be rich with the quirks, contradictions, and uniqueness that make up real human beings. Your job as the adaptor is to include and allow for the unexpected combination of traits that makes a character memorable, identifiable, and different from the other characters in this play or any other. Some of the most compelling conflicts to follow over the course of a play's action are characters' inner conflicts—the struggles within themselves that they seek to resolve.

One way to get a handle on whether the characters you are considering as the center of your adaptation have the richness to sustain a full evening's performance is to define their through-lines. To state through-lines for characters is to describe how they change as the play progresses. King Lear begins blind and arrogant and then comes to humility, as he sees what love and suffering are in others. Scrooge changes from cold, petty, and controlling to warm, generous, and open to experience. Here are character developments that can be tracked in the *Cockfighter* script.

Sonny   From idolizing his Dad to rebelling against him
Father   From tough and playful to brutally hard
Mother   From protective and scattered to enveloping
Homer   From on thin ice to falling through

Actors' Skill at Playing Multiple Roles

The sensation of *The Life and Adventures of Nicholas Nickleby* or *The Grapes of Wrath* on Broadway was partly the pleasure of watching an ensemble of actors playing multiple roles, painting a big-canvas world stroke by stroke. The changes of double-cast characters added resonant layers to the interlocking strands of story being told both dramatically and narratively.

In adapting *The Cockfighter*, I made a major decision: to restrict the casting to three actors. They played the essential roles culled from the novel: the boy, the father (played by the actor who also voiced the aggressive Tennessee handler), and the mother (played by an actress who also doubled as her brother Homer). This tight assignment of three actors playing thematically related characters kept the focus on the family bloodline and what Sonny would inherit from his mother's or father's side of the family. Elevating the secondary character of the uncle to pair with the mother (his sister) gave counterweight to the formidable scale of the father's presence in the material. It also helped get the play produced by limiting the number of actors the theaters had to hire.

This decision in *The Cockfighter* adaptation involved a significant trust in actors' transformational techniques. One actress playing both the mother and her brother Homer helps distill the roles by keeping us rooted in a familial triangle of father, son, and mother/uncle. In assessing what is gained or lost in this kind of casting choice, we kept the major focus on the family bloodlines competing to mold the boy, and those lines became dramatically stronger as we kept the audience attending to the mother-father conflict.

Example: An Actor's Transformation, Doubling Roles in The Cockfighter

The sequential monologues I gave to the mother and Homer enter each of their points of view by the actress switching characters, time, and place. During the following speech, adapted from eleven pages of text in the novel, the woman acting these two roles starts as Lily:

MOTHER: I didn't know that when I had a boy, I'd have to lose him. A daughter would be mine for the rest of my life, but if I had a boy, and I really loved him, I'd have to let him go. And not just now. I was going to have to do it over and over the rest of my life. (Pause.) One time at church the preacher said a woman had twins, and one of them died, but nobody knew it. The woman didn't even know it was twins. One was born, but the other one that died stayed up in her and never came out. The preacher said it turned into stone. Every little cell it had in its body turned into stone like a worm in the ocean that died a million years ago and fell to the bottom, and little by little it turned into stone. Later on, the woman got pregnant and had another baby, and that's how they found out. She passed it along with the other. It looked just like a regular baby. . . . (Brief pause.) It was just like meeting a total stranger and hearing him tell your whole life story up to and including the future. Pretty soon it would be as though they had walled me up inside. The whole thing will turn into stone. Not just the little baby inside me, like my own dearest twin, but my heart and my soul and my tender affections.

Pretty soon there won't be anything left except me, and inside me, if you broke me open, a perfect little petrified baby—like a jewel. . . . It will be mine, and it will always be with me—flesh of my flesh, bone of my bone. The great, sheltering wings of my pelvis will close in around it like valves of stone, protecting it from all harm until we become one thing: one man and one woman, one husband and one wife, one mother and one child. (130; see also the novel, 55–58)

The play then transitions into a new scene, which opens part III. At this point, the actress playing Lily sheds her flower print nightgown, revealing coveralls and T-shirt, transforming in body and voice in full view of the audience to become her brother Homer as he enters the cockfighting ring with Sonny. So the maternal line continues in dramatic opposition to the paternal line's efforts to shape the boy.

Later, after the defeated boy and father leave the cockfighting ring to head home, they drop recovering alcoholic Homer at a bar, where he talks to an unseen woman. This is the actress's last appearance as Homer:

HOMER: I said, you married? She said, Yeah, I used to be. That's how come I'm sitting here drinking. I got a bunch of marital troubles. . . . What you think about a boy lost his cock? You got any opinions on that? She said, Yeah. Lots of them. . . . My former husband had a cock, and I know for a fact he'd have been a whole lot better off if he didn't. I said, What if I told you it was a chicken? . . . Well, shit! Get him another. As soon as she said it, I knew what to do. I said, All right! Where do I get one? . . . How about you and me joining forces? She said, Doing what? I said, Looking for cock. She said, That's what I'm doing! I let out a whoop. . . . I felt like crowing, I was so happy. Whatever the boy lost in that cockfight, and whatever I lost when- ever I lost it, so long ago I can't even remember, the whiskey gave it back for a while, and it felt so good, I kept on drinking till I was too drunk to move. I woke up the next morning and saw the blank wash of light at the window and wondered how a man could lose so much, over and over and over again, and still have more to lose even after he lost it all. (148; see also the novel, 175–85)

This scene in part V is Homer's last appearance. When the actress appears again in part VI, and for the rest of the play, it is as Lily. Now the doubling of parts along a family bloodline has created a rich connec- tion between the characters, as Homer's inability to comprehend loss foreshadows Lily's similar inability to comprehend losing her son to the training rituals of the males in her life.

Acting is primarily about transformation—the ability of the actor to find the voice, body, costume, psychology, and emotional life of a character. Changing movement, tone, accent, clothing, or rhythm between characters lets an actor play both a seventy-year-old rabbi and a fortyish mom, as Meryl Streep did in *Angels in America*. Go to see any Shakespeare production and witness a few actors playing multiple roles.

While a novel can have as many characters as the author can create, in theater each actor adds to the payroll. The economics of hiring a limited number of actors can motivate the playwright to find ways to discover resonance in the story by having one actor play revealingly parallel roles. Whether driven by financial concerns that create unexpected discoveries or prompted by artistic choices that also happen to ease the budget, double casting can sometimes be revelatory. In a Royal Court production of *Hamlet,* Jonathan Pryce played both Hamlet and his father, with the father speaking through Hamlet as if the son were possessed. This production gave the audience an eye-opening insight into what a ghost could do to get his vengeance wrought through his son.

Letting Actors Shape Your Vision

Certain actors are able to convey subtle flavors or curious contradictions in the roles they create, say, between innocence and recklessness or in a character's blend of meekness and rage. Writing with a talented actor in mind can inspire your understanding of how to flesh out a character. But allow for the possibility that collaboration with a different actor, perhaps a radically different kind of actor, will then bring a whole new dimension to the role, an interpretation you hadn't imagined. There are well-known films for which the writer created a role with a certain actor in mind but found the part transformed with unexpected success when another actor was cast:

- *Beverly Hills Cop* was written with Arnold Schwarzenegger in mind. His unavailability eventually rolled the character over to Eddie Murphy, a decidedly different actor.
- Cameron Crowe wrote the screenplay for *Jerry Maguire* with Tom Hanks in mind as Jerry. Tom Cruise came into the casting late, wanting to play a loser character. Since Hanks projects solidity and decency and Cruise

Fig. 4. *Me and My Shadow*. Dueling personalities. (Bill McCann, Kathleen Patrick, Kirsten Giroux, Michael Atwell, and Tim McDonough, Theater Works, 1982.)

dazzle and invulnerability, the casting of Cruise shaped the ascent of emotional decency that the character acquires.

Each adaptor must make the call as to what proportion of competing character traits works for the adaptation. Perhaps your characters were so richly drawn in your original material that you already have a vivid sense of them, and they are unlike any person or actor you know. But if picturing a person or a particular actor playing one of your roles helps you to catch the rhythms of the character, then use that picture as you put together your script. Just be ready to release those choices to the vision of the director and actors who will shape them further.

Remember that character is a distillation of personality. Just as you cannot possibly capture every nuance of a living, breathing personality in your script, know that the actor who is cast will bring her unique personality and ineffable, indefinable qualities to fill in those spaces that the writing cannot. If you stay involved with your adaptation throughout its production, remain open to the delightful surprises that this aspect of collaboration can bring to your work.

Relationship: The Mortar That Holds Characters Together

Relationships are the key ingredient of great theater, and they are often complex and contradictory: two spouses who love each other can be in divorce court, a good boss can be hard on an admired employee, and siblings can cherish each other as they do disturbing things to each other. Dramatic relationships balance opposites: loving/hating, giving/taking, desiring/denying, telling/lying. Sometimes a plot is the story of a relationship, balancing perspective and emphasis between the two characters in it, rather than focusing on just one main character.

Character and conflict dominate our idea of theater. If well-defined characters are the engine of a dramatic event, then conflict is the fuel. Yet what often compels the audience is the connection between the characters—the relationship. For us to feel its endangerment, we first have to see the relationship that does or is trying to exist.

Relationships come with definable expectations, for example, that mothers and daughters will share secrets much as fathers and sons might pass a football. We expect lovers to kiss, a boss to criticize an employee, students to raise their hands when a teacher asks questions in class. Vital relationships expand the boundaries of how we understand what is possible between people. We discover what ties them together. After Rose loses her baby in *The Grapes of Wrath* yet finds the humanity to breast-feed a starving man, we encounter a new idea of mothering. The actions between people define the relationship and let us know what they want, need, demand, or can accept from each other.

Most relationships have discernible patterns of behavior that reveal what holds the two people together, what they want from each other, what they love about each other, or at least what they need from each other. What holds them in the relationship when conflict pushes at its seams? To dramatize these patterns, there are two significant methods for constructing a relationship. The first is by analogy: what is the relationship like? A mother-child relationship might be like (a) a wrestling match, (b) a strict teacher and an undisciplined student, or (c) a beautifully danced tango. Any of these parallels would unlock revealing behaviors that can be extrapolated into what the women play with each other.

The second construction method is based on observations, whether from personal experience of being in a mother-child pair, clues in the original text, or other sources such as literature or psychological studies, to define and devise actions that reveal those observations. Does the mother put the garbage bag in her absent daughter's chair, treating her like something foul and disposable, as anthropologist Jules Henry observed in his groundbreaking study of American families in the chapter "Pathways to Madness" in *Culture against Man*? Or do you remember the cooing comfort from your mom when she lovingly cleaned and bandaged your scraped knee? These are playable actions—which I will explore further in chapter 6—repeatable choices that reveal the nature of a specific mother-daughter interaction.

What makes the relationships in each story unique is not only their epoch and circumstances but also the vocabulary of expression the playwright or adaptor uses to communicate their specifics. In *King Lear*, there are over a hundred uses of the verb *to see*. This thematic through-line alone defines a world in which Cordelia is attempting to make her father see, while Lear nevertheless insistently avoids doing so. As you look for the threads that tie your characters together, be alert to the specifics of their language with each other that establish their unique relationship. Attend to the language style. Is the speaking flowery, with long baroque sentences and exotic word choices, as in a Restoration drama or Molière? Or is it truncated, flat, and brutal, as with David Mamet or F.X. Kroetz? Our grammar and word choices reveal our class, culture, and race. Also pay attention to any nonverbal patterns between the characters that establish their unique connections to each other. Behavior is theatrical vocabulary. You can include references to behaviors and patterns of behavior in the dialogue itself, as well as in stage directions.

Dramatically opposing traits can define one-on-one relationships, whether in or outside familial definition—friends, counselors, housemates, club members. In Neil Simon's *The Odd Couple*, two unrelated men are thrown together to live in a single apartment (one a neat freak, and one a slob), creating an archetypal relationship of contrasting traits. In the adapting of Michael Ondaatje's *Collected Works of Billy the Kid*, Tim McDonough and I contrasted a Billy who is boyish, impulsive, hot tempered, fun loving, and social against his nemesis Pat Garrett, who is mature, calculating, droll, cold, and a loner.

Family: The Blueprint for Understanding Relationship

Family is the prism through which we see and understand most relationships in our lives. Myriad, powerful alliances form: brother-sister, mother-father, mother-daughter, or father-son. Other widening circles tighten around grandparents, uncles, aunts, and cousins. As we move on to friends, enemies, and spouses, we often bring the definitions of family to those relationships to understand their effect on us: "I love him like a brother," "Stop acting like my mother," or "I hate my roommates, they're like the stepsisters in Cinderella."

Example: Declarations of Love Between Lear and His Daughter

When King Lear impulsively dismisses the honest Cordelia for not exaggerating her love for him, the relationship spirals downward until she reclaims him during the ensuing war. Finally, he must claim her murdered body. As he carries her onstage in the heartbreaking "howl, howl, howl" speech, not only does he feel grief and complicity, but part of him won't see that she is dead. Too many writers and actors focus on the grief and tears of such a scene. Great writing and acting allow the fuller *relationship* to have its unique voice: that two characters love each other but their character flaws—his pigheadedness and her inflated sense of honor—cripple their love for each other at critical moments. He is responsible for the circumstances that have led to her death, and while he holds her breathless body he believes he can feel her breathing. Shakespeare has written a very specific relationship with minimal stage time to define it. The clues in the text allow collaborators a lot of interpretive leeway in how benign or tempestuous this father-daughter relationship will be, but the through-line of the relationship is vividly drawn.

Example: Building the Mother-Daughter Relationship in The Grapes of Wrath

In *The Grapes of Wrath,* the vocabulary of expression in the mother-daughter relationship includes tough-love kitchen rituals. When Connie deserts his young pregnant wife, Rose of Sharon Joad, a confrontation ensues between Ma Joad and Rose in which the words, accompanied by the action of peeling with a knife, force Rose to face her situation:

ROSE OF SHARON: Where's Connie? I ain't seen Connie for a long time. Where'd he go?

MA: I ain't seen him. If I see 'em, I'll tell 'im you want 'im.

ROSE OF SHARON: I ain't feelin' good. Connie shouldn' of left me (*Ma looks at the girl's swollen face.*)

MA: You been a-cryin'. You git aholt of yaself. They's a lot of us here. Come here now an' peel some potatoes. You're feelin' sorry for yaself.

ROSE OF SHARON: He shouldn' of went away.

MA: You got to work. I ain't had time to take you in han'. I will now. You take this here knife an' get to them potatoes. (*Rose of Sharon takes knife from Ma and sits at the fire.*)

ROSE OF SHARON: Wait'll I see 'im. I'll tell 'im.

MA: He might smack you. You got it comin' with whinin' aroun' an' can-dyin' yaself. If he smacks some sense in you I'll bless 'im. (*Rose of Sharon's eyes blaze. Ma and Pa move away.*) (60–61)

Families often express a definable style of unique behavior. The Lear family in *King Lear,* the Joad family in *The Grapes of Wrath,* and the Cantrell family in *The Cockfighter* have parents and children who lock horns over youthful rebellion. The vocabulary of how it expresses itself—the alcoholic behavior of a Eugene O'Neill family, the self-righteousness of an Arthur Miller family, or the blunt violence in a Naomi Wallace clan—appears in specific habits they share and visit on each other.

Example: Generational Sparring in The Cockfighter

In *The Cockfighter* the vocabulary for the locked horns of youthful rebellion against the parents plays out at both a realistic and an imagistic level. A world set in a cockfighting ring guided the actors to relationship moments that suggested human actions akin to cockfighting. Sonny would at times recoil from the harsh demands of his father and the smothering nurture of his mother Lily. We would literalize the actions: a father's sudden lunge like a cock in flight at a fight, a mother's enveloping hug like a bird spreading its wings, a boy's recoiling from either parental action like a wounded bird running and hitting the edge of the enclosed hog wire pit.

In the following passage, the father belittles Sonny's nurturing gestures toward his chickens.

FATHER: (*as* SONNY *nuzzles his pet "Lion"*) Get away from that cock, goddamn it! You don't want them to get used to you. Standing there
with your thumb up your ass looking at them like it was a girl showing her tits, they turn into chickens. (127)

In passages like these, the characters of *The Cockfighter* came alive for
me in the uniqueness and specificity that Manley had written for them.

Characters and relationships are essential to building an adaptation.
These are the people you will live with for months and your audience
will discover within minutes. You want to be as specific and evocative as
possible about their traits, language, actions, and interactions with others and their world.

✦ ✦ ✦ ✦

CONSTRUCTION EXERCISES FOR BUILDING BLOCK 3

Knowing your principal characters will give you a wide array of materials to
shape the construction of your adaptation. Now you can begin to build a
three-dimensional portrait of your primary character. Fill in the following exercises where you can. If you have two equally important main characters, work
through the exercises for each of them.

For Character
A. Decide who is the pivotal character in the play.
B. Articulate for yourself what this character wants and needs most. Does he
    or she get it?
C. In twenty words, how would you describe your pivotal character to
    someone who doesn't know the book? State the arc of his or her story.
    Hamlet goes from being depressed and inactive to being engaged in
    actions, almost an action hero. How does your principal character change
    throughout the story?
D. What are the most important actions that involve this character: actions
    that provoke important events, change the course of the story and move
    things forward? Cite four major actions that happen to this character.
    How does he or she react? Then cite four of this character's own major
    actions or decisions.
E. List the essential character traits for your principals. Circle their three
    most likable and unlikable qualities.

F. Study your cut-and-paste draft of scenes that you have chosen for your adaptation. What character traits are diminished by what you cut out of the larger work? Which are emphasized?

G. Test your knowledge of and connection to your main character. To find the character traits in the source material, consider yourself a detective and highlight the character clues in the text. Start as factually as possible.
    • What does the character say about himself or herself?
    • What do the characters say about each other?
    • What does the narrator say about the character?
    • And are these distortions, lies, and exaggerations or reliable descriptions of character traits?

H. Also from the original text, take notes on passages that indicate
    • How the characters look (clothes, makeup)
    • Physical objects they use (cane, backpack, carving knife)
    • How they appear physically (stance, height, movement style, rhythm)
    • Their voice (accent, pitch, soft or loud)
    • Their language style (sentence shape, grammar and word choices)
    • Their psychology (fears, wants, most present emotions, foibles)

I. Examine the scenes you've chosen for your cut and paste. Is there enough embedded in your selections to uncover a richly layered portrait of who your characters are?

J. Do some research for ideas on your main character. Find pictures that remind you of a certain character or information about the people of a certain era or culture.

K. For secondary characters that will be less developed, who often exist only to advance a story point or enhance the theme, write down two to three traits. For example, the used car salesmen in *The Grapes of Wrath* are slick, friendly, and dressed in shabby suits. To better know a secondary character you are creating, you might work up a full character profile. More often, given that you have less to work with, it will be enough for you to cite three traits that define how they operate in the world.

L. If a scheme for doubling characters suggests itself or if your adaptation requires some doubling, look for thematic connections between the characters. For instance, some productions of *King Lear* double the Fool and Cordelia, as they are both truth tellers in the play and don't appear in any scenes together. Or look for practical physical parallels to guide double-casting decisions: are there two characters roughly matched in age or gender?

For Relationship

M. What is the most important relationship in your adaptation? Who are these characters to each other?

N. Note all specific text references to what happens between the characters that define the relationship. What are the two or three most important actions that involve both of them?

O. What is the relationship analogous to? What is it like? (For example, Maggie and Brick in *Cat on a Hot Tin Roof* are like a Persian cat and a bulldog fighting.)

P. Note all text references for imaginative or metaphorical relationship choices, such as *The Cockfighter* characters as fighting cocks.

Q. As you prepare to consider questions about storyline for the next chapter, consider your primary relationships and define who is struggling with whom. Where is the greatest tension between characters in the adaptation? What is their central conflict? What is the glue that holds them together in spite of this tension?

R. Read out loud the entire text that you've selected for your adaptation. Do you sense from the language that the stakes of the various characters and their personalities are different?

S. Choose a scene that is focused on character or relationship and write your adaptation version of it.

You know you have completed this building block when you get excited about and can visualize your main character. Tell the character's story and journey through the play to a friend. Keep it simple, as if you were introducing a good friend and wanted to give a quick overview of this part of the character's life. Don't judge: if you have characters like Iago from *Othello,* we may not like their behaviour, even if we are fascinated by what could be motivating them and how their actions change the lives of those they love. Your task at this stage is to describe and define who they are, withholding moral qualms to explore later, as your adaptation and the production evolve.

The previous chapter concluded with your reading the scene-by-scene template that you culled from your source to create your adaptation. Now you are beginning to find its voices. No longer the omniscient or single authorial voice of the original text, the voice of your adaptation is becoming a complex chorus of points of view as you eliminate, combine, or create characters in order to balance dialogue, narrative, and theme. Now you are ready to delve into the wild card element of imagery.

4 ⋆ *Building Block Four*

Choose an Evocative Stageable Image

Theater exists in the three-dimensional present. When we experience great theater, it can be a production of Thorton Wilder's *Our Town* in a high school auditorium, where the searing innocence shines through; the Broadway musical *Chicago* with its sassy sexuality; or Franca Rame's *Tomorrow's News* in an experimental space in the bowels of a boiler room, where we can bear witness to state terrorism. When we experience it, what ignites our connection is both a personal relationship with the material and an active interplay of stage, audience, and actor. The actor in front of us is often our biggest focus and strongest memory of a theatrical event. What contextualizes the event is knowing *where* the thing is happening. And our careful attention to where we grew up, where we lost our virginity, went to school, got married, or felt the presence of God, testifies to the deeply ingrained physical memory that place conjures for us.

The environment is the wild card element in an adaptation; it can add an unexpected dimension. You know that most novels have specific places in which the character likes to work and play. Theater often evokes these places using imaginative methods, so that the story can stay focused on the people and not on design elements that will upstage the actors. Often one location will stand out; it's the place where the central event happens or the conflict occurs.

The theme is the essential floor of the adaptation you're constructing. If we accept the design as the roof of the world your characters inhabit, then finding the evocative stageable image is having your feet grounded on that floor and reaching for the ceiling. Your intellectual and artistic challenge is to imagine how to fuse what the story is about— the theme—with where it happens: the locations from your adaptation. How do these two meet where your characters will live?

Finding the Theatrical Environment

Staging is the term for the arrangement of actors onstage, for where and how they move. It is primarily actors that animate the theater space, by using their bodies and voices. Lighting, scenery, props, and sound scoring add support in varying degrees. Plays and adaptations face decisions about the visual world in which the actors will realize their characters. To work, staging needs a resonant sense of place, of where.

Environment gives us the context within which our lives unfurl. Most stage sets, even within the limited confines of a theatrical stage, are realistic: a kitchen, a dark street corner, the edifice of a college entranceway, a bed, or an altar can all be re-created on a stage. For practical and financial reasons, theater must be quite selective as to what it shows in the stage setting. In a literary adaptation, in which characters and language often dominate, we usually need to have a specific idea for the onstage environment of the piece. Using the play's theme to help you imagine a space that will work metaphorically is a vital technique for shaping an evocative environment that will also work practically with your adaptation.

A metaphoric space is suggestive, evocative, and detailed enough to suggest the larger world that encompasses the play. Balancing the play's theme with the practical needs of staging actors and objects on a stage will uncover the idea for such a space. An evocative stageable metaphor should have a sense of location and theme built into it. To evoke the husband theatrically in my first production of Samuel Beckett's "Enough," the woman's hands animated his size-twelve shoes. One sequence of my staging had her creating a syncopated walk with the shoes played against her marching in place. In *The Grapes of Wrath* the wildly varied laundry suspended on a clothesline across a Broadway stage was enough to conjure a massive squatter's camp.

It usually takes a knowledgeable scenic designer to do a great design for an adaptation. Designers are familiar with different architectural spaces, from Broadway-style prosceniums to thrust stages, blackboxes, and found spaces. Others who can think innovatively about ways to use space, such as a visual artist or an architect, might also do good design work. It helps to have a designer who also has some sense of what actors need and production timetables. You may even get the opportunity to work with a scenographer in the tradition of Josef Svoboda, a designer who is involved in creating the whole world of a production and takes a holistic approach by incorporating text, director's ideas, and conceptual initiatives. A workable adaptation will give your designer an idea of what imaginative place it could be played in. Your staging metaphor will guide the design choices.

We all have some experience of arranging space to suit our needs and others'. Where we place a table in our kitchen, arrange couches in our living room, or set up a picnic area for a family Fourth of July—all these choices define how and where we move when we interact. By surveying the locations of the scenes you have been selecting for your adaptation and seeing where the locations overlap, you can condense the number of set elements needed, thereby guiding a set designer. The most concise condensing will carry you to an overarching theatrical environment that incorporates most or all the locations in your adaptation and builds on a possible stageable image. In this way you give a designer leads and images with which to work. Finding literal details in the novel that can become a stageable image—such as the cockpit in *The Cockfighter*—allows you to build around it as you use other specific locations in your adaptation.

Contemporary Staging:
Spatial Metaphors as Viable Playing Spaces

Current producing pressures force most new scripts to stay under two hours running time, with a small cast that includes a local or national celebrity if the show hopes to run more than five weeks. Literary adaptations tend to follow the current model of scripted plays. Expensive production values meant to dazzle an audience paying top-dollar ticket prices often overwhelm the story, characters, and intent of the play. An example of such a production cost is the angel in *Angels in America,* which was a theatrical blast through the ceiling of a house on Broadway and in the regional theaters but was more moving and germane to the story when played simply on a ladder in the National Theatre of London production.

The Life and Adventures of Nicholas Nickleby was a production that shattered most of the rules. David Edgar's extraordinary two-part adaptation of this Charles Dickens novel, which was one of the great comic masterpieces of the nineteenth century, became a landmark production not just for the Royal Shakespeare Company but also for the British theater on its premier in 1980. The very commitment to deliver a literary adaptation of a weighty Dickens novel to the stage drove the company to bring innovations to the theater, including an eight-and-a-half-hour running time, a large cast (42 performers playing 138 speaking roles), and hundred-dollar ticket prices, plus multiple plotlines and a profusion of language.

Trevor Nunn and John Caird directed a production that evoked multiple environments of nineteenth-century London within the stageable image of an industrial warehouse. This primary set permitted within it the creation of multiple locations, which could be defined by single elements that allowed fluid transitions between scenes: a wooden bench, a fancy chair, a street lamp, and a chandelier. On a thematic level, this setting also evoked Dickens's theme of the dehumanizing aspects of the Industrial Revolution in England, when bosses shackled workers to repetitive, machinelike jobs.

As an hour-long monologue, my version of Samuel Beckett's "Enough" was another adaptation that broke the rules. In this story, its theme being the escape provided by memory, a woman takes a step and remembers. Creating the piece with great collaborators, I found an evocative stageable image that inspired three different and richly suggestive designs, of which you'll find detailed descriptions in chapter 8. Student designers created the inspired set for the piece's first incarnation.

John Barth's story "Petition" is exactly that, a written petition to the King of Siam from the rear half of Siamese twin brothers, and its theme of conflicted duality plays out in the physically connected brothers. What allowed these and most literary adaptations to move from the page to the stage was a clear theme made manifest in a theatrical space by a stageable metaphor. The key image teases out what is theatrically embedded in the text and what is possible onstage. It allows the visual, three-dimensional realization of the theme.

Contemporary plays have opened up starched-collar conventions of nineteenth-century naturalism and then gone beyond them with startling metaphoric treatments. In the insightful National Theatre of England's production of J. B. Priestley's *An Inspector Calls,* a tiny, floating house cracks open to make the inhabitants vulnerable to the war around them, a war represented in rich impressionistic details, including both sound and light. And for its long Broadway run, Michael Blakemore directed an inspired production of *Copenhagen,* by Michael Frayn, to be performed as if bodies were at times atoms, spiraling and colliding. The piece followed through on its evocative stageable image not only in its set but also in its actors' physical character choices.

Fig. 5. *The Collected Works of Billy the Kid.* Mythic Billy the Kid and Pat Garrett meet. (David Perrigo and Tim McDonough, Reality Theater, 1978.)

Evocative Details: Parts Suggest the Whole

The adaptation of literature to the stage has the potential, and some-times the need, to invent anew. As the most realistic performing art, with real people in real time, theater is paradoxically also one of the most symbolic. A few men represent an army in *Richard III,* a desk a fully appointed office in *Nicholas Nickleby,* a tree the natural world in Beckett's *Waiting for Godot.* In suspending our disbelief about the scale of the physi-cal world, we are reinvesting in the invisible world of spirituality, emo-tion, subjective perception, dream, fantasy, and imagination. We let the theater imply all the realistic environments that film depicts or fiction describes. We trust the audience to be as imaginative, intelligent, and open-minded as the company creating the work. Although the adaptor and collaborators must till the soil to seed a well-told story, the crops are harvested in the mind, emotions, and personal experience of each audience member.

Example from The Grapes of Wrath *of an Effective Staging Metaphor*

The Grapes of Wrath family's journey from the Dust Bowl of Oklahoma to the promised land of California during the Great Depression had a tough, documentary-like visual treatment in the John Ford film. The script for the stage adaptation of the story eschews the descriptive chapters of the novel, instead taking key narration and assigning it to several minor characters as the method to keep us connected to the tumult in the Joad family journey. Frank Galati chose a distilled, symbolic staging, with the evocative stageable image of a spare, bereft Dust Bowl that engenders human compassion. The play took the empty stage as the Dust Bowl and employed natural elements such as fire, water, and dirt to suggest the terrain that the single, battered truck traversed. Only essential elements would appear—a tent, a stool, a clothesline, a pot on a fire— leaving the focus on the actors playing the Joads, as the members of the family and their possessions were torn or siphoned from the lone car that symbolically carried them on the journey. In the published script, Galati explained his approach: "Our efforts in designing the play were always to make the most modest use of available stagecraft. We strove to be simple. Simplicity is difficult to achieve and sometimes the expressive power of stage effects can overtake story and character" (8).

In the film version, the ranging eye of the camera created the vast Dust Bowl plains, the thousands caught in squatter's camps, the abandoned homes, the piled-up automobiles, and the flood. What theater does better is to allow us to experience, in the real time of performance, the living history of the Joad family—a history we share in watching families break apart with the stress of relocating. The courage, love, and spiritual strength of the Joads, tested by natural calamity and predatory human nature, is the human story Galati reveals. His adaptation builds its imagery around the relationship of the family.

Imagining Onstage:
Setting the Scene with What's Necessary and Evocative

In transferring a literary work to the stage, you must acknowledge the limitations and strengths of live theater. Yes, some popular ideas of stage design suggest that, at least on Broadway, spectacle rules. But for most adaptations to best tell the story and be playable for the actors, the adaptor needs to think imaginatively about the environment. Peter Brook explains this unique quality of live theater beautifully in his book *The Empty Space.*

> ... the absence of scenery in the Elizabethan theatre was one of its greatest freedoms. . . . the cinematic structure of alternating short scenes, plot intercut with subplots, were all part of the total shape. This shape is only revealed dynamically, that is, in the uninterrupted sequence of these scenes. . . .
>
> Compared to the cinema's mobility, the theater once seemed ponderous and creaky, but the closer we move towards the true nakedness of theater, the closer we approach a stage that had a lightness and range far beyond film or television. (86–87)

Film and TV are full of numerous realistic details. Theater, less literal in its design elements, allows the audience to imagine the larger environments inspired by selected, revealing details. The symbolic nature of theatrical space heightens the focus on the actors. When I directed *Death of a Salesman,* our dramaturgical research on Arthur Miller unearthed an architect's floor plan of a house in Brooklyn. Inspired by the idea of such a house, the designer laid out a blueprint on the stage floor in scale. Selected furniture placed on top of it, such as a kitchen table or a desk for the office, was all the audience needed in order to know where they were.

In finding a workable environment for the set design of an adaptation, one must often go outside the traditional box of decorative scenic designs and envision something new. Your job as the adaptor is to point your designer in the right direction and to have thought about the metaphorical resonances of the locations you choose for your scenes in ways that can inspire their creativity.

Sometimes the new is based on the old, such as the Elizabethan-style open stage with minimal furniture and props employed by *The Grapes of Wrath* and *Nicholas Nickleby* to suggest their multiple locations. On *The Cockfighter*'s open stage, cages functioned as chairs and other furniture pieces, an automobile, or steps. Your adaptation is the designer's guide to possible environments, which in turn create staging possibilities for the director and playable spaces for the actors.

In three very different productions of *Enough,* three different designs sprang from the same adaptation script: one by a painter/sculptor, the second by a scenographer, and the third by an expansive-thinking theater designer. If you stay attuned to the visual and metaphoric dimension of your play, you can inspire a wide range of creative possibilities for your collaborators, who can reveal the latitude one has as an adaptor for imagining the text onto a stage.

Creative Spaces

Actors could have stood at the front of the stage and read *Nicholas Nickleby* for the nine hours it took to perform it, but I suspect a long run and BBC television version wouldn't have followed. In a fruitful interplay between playwriting and design, experiments in theatrical form prompt new styles of writing, and, conversely, experiments with language also drive collaborating theater artists to experiment with other new forms. By its nature, literary adaptation, in moving from one medium to another, requires flexible strategies for how to best realize the work in a theatrical context.

The environmental theater movement, for instance, expanded notions of possible venues for performances, including literary adaptations. Squat Theater created theatrical events by converting the found space of a storefront on 23rd Street in New York City. The production incorporated the sight of pedestrians walking past the storefront windows, in full view of the audience inside, and made them part of the story. Mary Zimmerman staged *Metamorphoses* in a swimming pool for the Lookingglass Theater in Chicago. Theater without Theater was a joint project of the Canadian Arts Lab and Peter Froehlich, chair of theater at the University of Ottawa. They set out to turn the liability of a fire-destroyed theater and a lack of facilities into an advantage. They staged environmental advocacy pieces in the Ottawa Canal, mystery pieces in malls, and Eugene O'Neill's *Before Breakfast* at 7:00 a.m. in a neighborhood kitchen.

In the company I cofounded early in my career, Theater Works, in Boston, we staged *Living in Exile,* a retelling of *The Iliad,* in homes around the city, employing ordinary lamps and candles for light and seating the audience on couches. Touchstone Theatre in Vancouver staged its wild, spooky *Haunted House Hamlet* in mansions across Canada. The audience followed different characters into various rooms of plot and subplot and met occasionally to share the various strands of the story. Environmental theater also brought the natural world into theater venues: tons of sand for a retelling of the Saul and David story in *Beginner's Luck,* or graveyard dirt and Joseph Cornell–inspired assemblages in wooden boxes for *The Collected Works of Billy the Kid,* both of which I directed for Boston's Reality Theater in the 1970s.

Choosing and Integrating an Evocative Stageable Image

Adaptors take the imaginative leap to the stageable scenic images by attending to the location clues in their adapted literature. Cueing from literal locations and images in the original stories, adaptors each imagined workable metaphoric spaces where the following stories could unfold:

- *Nicholas Nickleby:* an industrial warehouse
- "Enough"*:* the landscape of a man's body
- *Billy the Kid:* a Joseph Cornell–like collage box
- "Petition"*:* a circus sideshow
- *Crow:* twelve-foot black silk wings for the actor
- *Black Witness:* a shattering church window
- *Pathways to Madness:* white gurneys and hospital masks

Example from The Cockfighter*:*
Establishing a Location and Finding Evocative Visual Details

The Cockfighter might be more electrifying if staged in the hundreds of legal and illegal cockfighting pits that exist around the world. (In fact a busy tour of Brooklyn could be arranged where dozens of unsanctioned cockpits exist.) As it was, the initial workshop production of *The Cockfighter,* developed at Theater Emory and coproduced with PushPush Theater at its adventurous warehouse in Atlanta, was set in a replica of a cockfighting ring as described in the novel.

> At one end of the main pit was a gate made of wood and wire and a chair for the scorekeeper. It looked like a lifeguard's chair at the beach. It had slats nailed to the side so the scorekeeper could climb up. . . . The bleachers were shaped like a V. They came down on either side of the pits, and the rake was so steep they looked like ledges of rock going straight up a cliff all the way from the floor to the ceiling. The seats and the framing were made of rough

lumber—unpainted, unplaned oak planks a full two inches thick, cut at a jackleg sawmill nearby. (79–80)

The audience walked under the distressed board bleachers down a thin corridor and encountered signs, also as described in the novel.

Pit rules
Everybody pays
Absolutely no Drinking
Anyone Drinking will be Barrd
Watch your Language
Keep your Bets Straight
Weigh in by 10:00
All Derbies Blind Matchd
Once Enterd in Derby you Can Not Withdraw
Absolutely no flat gaffs
No Quick or rough Handling
Anyone Buying, Selling a Fight
Or Switching Bands will
Be Barrd
Worthman rules used (78)

Once in the environment, the audience found colorful quilts strewn on highly raked benches, facing hog wire, surrounding an acting space with a red earth floor and another triangle-shaped slice of the benches facing back at them.

This ritual, rough environment invited the audience into the world of cockfighting at both a realistic and a symbolic level. It allowed the adaptation to focus on language, character, relationships, and the visual tug-of-war between the father and the mother/uncle over the son.

Wire mesh separated the watching audience from the family. The play is like a cockfight, staged with the father, son, and mother/uncle as humans with cockfighting qualities. Seated in tiers like the audience, the boy often between his parents, the actors together created a Shiva-like image, suggesting one body with multiple arms and legs, at times in silhouette. When they voiced the sounds of the birds or played actions of fluttering, pecking, or the stillness of a cock before lunging into battle, they metamorphosed from a human family into fighting cocks. My adaptation gave the designer the evocative stageable image of cocks fighting in a ring, and he fleshed out the idea with playable visual details that made it work onstage.

I had a wide range of inspiration for this style, from George Bernard Shaw's *Don Juan in Hell* to Samuel Beckett's *Play*, the emblematic acting style of the Open Theater, and the anthropomorphic characters of *Cats* and *The Lion King*. These plays sample a history of diverse writing and acting styles that influenced my ideas about the possibilities in realizing *The Cockfighter*. The spare, stripped-down language in *Play* and the rich, complex sentences of *Don Juan*, both done in a presentational style that made listening and character paramount, influenced what text I chose for my adaptation. They also shaped how I imagined an audience would receive the work. And what I learned from the non-naturalistic acting style of the Open Theater, as well as the animal-influenced performances in the Broadway musicals *Cats* and *Lion King*, opened up the notions I had about the actors' physical possibilities and character work.

Using Narration from a Character's Point of View to Establish Place

We are told in *The Tempest* that Ariel is invisible, and presto: he is. Theater's ability to call on the imagination of the audience points toward the vocal painting that a character can accomplish with striking stageworthy narration from literature.

Example of Characters Creating a Sense of Place in The Cockfighter

To establish the geography of the cockfighting pits, as well as the crowd that is there to witness and bet on the matches, I distilled the following speeches from those same few pages of narration in the novel. I assigned the first of two short descriptive monologues to the boy, who is entering this world expecting to emerge a man. The second went to Homer, his uncle, whose job for the dad is to keep track of which gamblers to hustle for bets. I chose the most active language of the passage, language that described the unseen people of the scene around the ring.

> BOY: We checked the pits. It had a dirt floor and was fenced in with hog wire three or four feet high. At one end of the main pit were a gate and a chair for the scorekeeper.
> HOMER: The bleachers were already filling up. The men had on jeans and field jackets and camouflage hunting clothes. They looked like a unit in a rebel army somewhere in Central America. (135)

Having made some visual details concrete in the set design—the drag pits, hog wire, and quilts—this vocal painting allowed us to create other details in the audience's imagination, such as the two other pits, the gate, and the women.

How Scale of Venue Changes the Focus

Size matters. In Hollywood vernacular, small films cost under thirty million, are E. M. Forster classics made by Merchant-Ivory, and have a niche market whose numbers won't allow the producers' profits to bail out Wall Street. Big films star computer-generated robots, cost over a hundred million to make, and allow the writer-director to say he is king of the world at the Academy Awards. In the more human-scaled arena of theater, the size of the venue, budget, and cast are important considerations in how you shape the adaptation. Sharing a live event most often suggests keeping the venue intimate.

Théatre de Complicité's Simon McBurney advocates a theater that makes the event of the adaptation present "not just a book that one person picks up and looks at, or film, which just reduces it to the essential elements of the story. But to share the presence of it with 500 people like a kind of celebration or party. If theater can make good parties, everyone will want to go."

Both *The Grapes of Wrath* and *Nicholas Nickleby* were successful in the celebration of theater's visceral storytelling ability, even in Broadway's thousand-plus-seat venues. Atypically, both were commissioned for specific spaces and by terrific acting companies capable of filling larger theaters. Most adaptations take place in fifty- to three-hundred-seat theaters of varying architectural conventions. One standard design is the traditional proscenium, through which all the audience members view the action from the same angle, looking at the front of the stage. Another is a more modern thrust stage, around which the audience sits on three sides of the action. In a Greek-inspired arena theater, the audience sits 360 degrees around the center playing space and is very aware of others in the audience watching. And in an Elizabethan playhouse such as the Black Rose at Theater Emory, people sit or stand in front of the stage, on the sides at stage level, and above it, looking down onto the actors from directly over them, as we might have imagined the nobility doing during the premier of *King Lear*. If you know what sort of space your adaptation will be playing in, that may guide some of your choices, your sense of reasonable possibilities. Even more important, to create a piece that inspires great design is to stay aware of your theme and choose an image that is strong enough to translate to a range of different kinds of spaces.

A venue sometimes leads to expanding or contracting the staging metaphor. By the time of the premier of *The Cockfighter* at the Actors Theatre of Louisville's Humana Festival of New American Plays, the earlier experiments in Atlanta had led to a spatial staging metaphor of family as cockfight. Moving from the highly intimate 80-seat PushPush Theater in Atlanta to a much larger 330-seat in-the-round space in Louisville changed the production focus of the adaptation. The arena of Louisville's Bingham Theater is architecturally reminiscent of most cockfighting rings. The theater even reminded me of a small arena space on a farm in Indonesia where I once witnessed a cockfight.

The Bingham's larger volume and 360-degree playing space required an acting style that didn't create the same stage pictures as the Atlanta thrust stage production had; the demands for vocal production required more movement, bigger acting choices, and less reliance on the language. So, with more accomplished actors, designers, and technical support, the production was more theatrical, both visually and aurally. This version intensified the impact of the archetypal, biological tug-of-war between the parents trying to shape the destiny of their son. The more intimate Jory Theater at Actors Theatre, comparable to the thrust stage used in Atlanta, might have elicited the rougher, in-your-face production in which the text would have remained focal. Instead the production in Louisville shifted the balance among the elements and became a much more character-driven performance. But the image of a cockfighting ring as representative of the relationships in the story, viscerally visual and deeply rooted as it was in the theme of the piece, held up beautifully through that shift in emphasis.

The primary setting for your adaptation, incorporating your key evocative stageable image, may already be obvious to you by now. If so, the following exercises will help you to check your choice to be sure it works well. And if you are still looking for that image and primary setting, the exercises can help you to find the metaphor that captures your theme and encapsulates it in a physical form that works for your space.

✦ ✦ ✦ ✦

CONSTRUCTION EXERCISES FOR BUILDING BLOCK 4

Start by scanning your source material, your notes on it from other chapters, and your cut-and-paste draft, which should now be filling out with finished scenes if you're working through the building blocks in order.

A. Remember what you found most powerful in your original source material. What is your stated theme?

B. Find three examples of language that leaves sensory impressions. Are there descriptive passages of the physical world of the play that you find resonant?

C. What about your characters evokes environments? Remember your work as a detective for the construction exercises on character in chapter 3, and highlight clues that connect to images. What places are most powerful for your key characters?

D. Refer to the scenes you have already chosen to include. Go through them, scene by scene, and list all the places you plan to include in your adaptation, noting which are most important. Notice when certain scenes must take place in certain locations because the place is integral to the scene. This may not be as often as you think, so consider how some scenes could be staged elsewhere and still make sense.

E. Thinking scene by scene, list all the essential furniture and major props that you know you need in your adaptation. (This list may change later as you get clearer about your imagery.)

F. Research: on the web or at a library find photos or artwork of the locations relevant to your adaptation. (In *The Grapes of Wrath* this would include roads, a campground, or a 1930s car.)

G. Now close your eyes to imagine three key scenes in one of your locations. Use one of your research photos of environments, if you have one. (In *The Grapes of Wrath,* possible environments would include the car, a road, and a campground; in *A Christmas Carol,* they would include a Victorian office, a bedroom, and the meager table of the Cratchits' Christmas dinner.)

• State your theme several times as you visualize a location and consider possible connections between that foundation and this image.

• In your imagination, try to see what your principal characters would *do* in that place. If you have written these key scenes or can use dialogue from the original novel, read the text of five to seven lines around these three important moments as you imagine the scenes. This is staging. It will reveal how flexible and useful the space is to actors playing actions.

H. Answer the following.
- What space gave you the most to work with?
- What specific actions did your characters play?
- What location gives you options for staging important events from different scenes? Where is there an overlap or parallel that facilitates combining the environments into one or just a few?
- Is there a place to which your imagination just jumped that is not on your location list in "C" above? What options does it give you for staging the important events?
- Based on your answers so far, choose the best setting for staging.

I. Name your evocative stageable image, keeping in mind your best setting location and most resonant detail. What image best captures the sense of your theme and is also playable in your stage environment?

J. Write at least one scene for your adaptation using your evocative stageable image to guide you as you choose the locations and key props. A good starting point is to look for a passage in your source that provides great descriptive language about your central image. Write dialogue that adapts this language into a dynamic, playable scene.

I hope the challenge of uncovering an evocative stageable image has been both fun and a muscle-building exercise for your three-dimensional imagination. As you have sifted through the facts—the named locations in your source text—and your associations with the images and imagined environments conjured in your mind, you have focused on the key clues to finding potential places for your scenes to play onstage. These can guide you in shaping your adaptation and your set designer in physically creating a workable sense of space.

5 ✦ *Building Block Five*

Construct the Storyline

As John Barth puts it, "The story of our life is not our life, it is our story." Just as personality is too immense to define but character can and must be captured to be playable, so constructing a storyline involves making choices as you build your script. Even a play based on a biography cannot include everything about a person's life, nor can you include every event from even a short novel in an evening of theater. The building block of storyline is about learning which events to keep and which to cut.

Defining the storyline of the literature you're adapting, using a theme you've chosen, is an important step in giving you a focus for what should move from the page to the stage. I encourage anyone working on an adaptation to distill the story down to one simple declarative sentence. Even when the story is immense, as in *Hamlet* or a Dostoyevsky, Dickens, or Alice Walker novel, state the story as you would to an eight year old. This is not to trivialize the material but to challenge yourself to say what is happening in its simplest form. You need a strong anchor to proceed with the art of adaptation, and the storyline is an invaluable place to secure adaptation structures. By the end of this chapter you will have that simple statement.

If you are working through the steps in the order I've presented them, then you now know your main theme, the scenes you want to include, your primary characters, and your evocative stageable image. These will shape your choices about the arc of your storyline. In this chapter we will delve into the main conflicts in those relationships, identify the central event of the story and key scenes, and determine what prior circumstances are essential to understanding your characters' story. If you begin this chapter uncertain of your theme or what the key relationships are, your work on the storyline should help you to finally define them. There is a fruitful interplay between the building blocks in which one can help you clarify another. And, within this chapter, finding a central event can point you toward naming a main conflict that has potentially eluded you. Conversely, having a clear notion of what the main conflict is can help you to find the central event, since it is the actual moment when the conflict shifts decisively.

To find the play in a work of literature, one must first come to terms with the principal building blocks of both literary and dramatic forms: the story and the theme. A story strings together events with a suggested beginning, middle, and end. The story is all the events and actions we can see or infer. The theme helps us see what the story is about—why it moves us and should be told to others.

Building a Storyline on Your Foundational Theme

Laurence Olivier intones at the beginning of his *Hamlet* film, "This is the story of a man who could not make up his mind." Olivier is guiding us, in such a reductive-sounding storyline of a monumental work, toward the theme of indecision. He is focusing thematically on Hamlet's indecision, his oscillation, and his need, ultimately, to make a choice. The text clearly establishes Olivier's context for exploring this theme in its "O that this too, too solid flesh would melt" and "To be or not to be." There are adaptations and cuttings of *Hamlet* that focus on Ophelia or Rosencrantz and Guildenstern, but Lawrence Olivier's theme of "a man who could not make up his mind" places the story firmly on the character of Hamlet, the conflicted prince.

Your success in this building block will be in having a storyline that acts as a sturdy framework for the myriad materials you can use to build the adaptation. There is a temptation to try to squeeze all aspects of the story into your one declarative sentence. But for Oliver to telescope Hamlet down into a man who could not make up his mind temporarily sets aside the intricate politics, the blood rivalry, the love story, and the madness. These can be added onto the solid frame of the character's journey. Learning more about the characters and structure may change your storyline as you write your adaptation. But do formulate a statement of your storyline by the time you work through this chapter. As you gather your materials, it is easier to go from one thing to another—from your best idea of the story to a better idea—than from only a collection of uncertain possibilities. A clear statement gives you strong supporting walls.

The same story can be told in many different ways—the politics of the Middle East, the reign of Elizabeth I, the idea of the nuclear family—all of which have had their stories told multiple times, altered by the theme of the storyteller. A telling of the Kennedy family's story could focus on their birthplace, heroism in wars, the web of family relationships, election to public office, marriages, parent-child tensions, assassinations, and the private aftermath of public events or specific people—whether Jackie, Robert, Ted, or John Jr. Any of these approaches could provide a foundation for a playable storyline. The arrangement and construction of events and actions shape the story in a perceivable structure, which, in turn, complicates and resolves as the story unfolds. Using your chosen theme to drive those choices makes your story work.

Conflict: Tensions between Characters That Add Heat and Light

The derivation of the word *drama* is "to seek and struggle." In the seeking and struggling, what defines characters is the conflict they face. What forces oppose them? To be in opposition to one's society, primary relationships, or self is to face conflict. To conflict is to clash, to fight for supremacy, to come into opposition. A conflict is a collision of opinions or interests, an inner moral struggle.

Theater allows us to bear witness to the conflicts that we have experienced or fear to encounter; it allows us to step outside the emotional chaos of the clash and see it with more discerning eyes. The great conflicts—human against God, human against nature, human against society, human against human, human against self—reverberate in the tangible stories we tell ourselves. We need the stories to put our conflicts in relief and to give us relief from them, so that we can hold them for a while, then put them away until they call to us again.

In literary adaptations, the inherent complication of making a stageworthy play is in heightening the conflict to sustain the tension. In characters' journey through a story, obstacles they meet define the conflict, and how they do or don't overcome those obstacles creates the events of the plot. This journey, a through-line of actions that can be played physically by an actor, creates the structure that will hold the adaptation together. By action we mean something characters can do to others or themselves that provokes a response, another action.

Hamlet's journey involves several objectives and a through-line of actions in which he takes revenge on those implicated in his father's death. He first must wake himself from "resolving into a dew" to actively challenge his stepfather, mother, girlfriend, college buddies, and others, in order to avenge the father who haunts him. First Hamlet wants to melt and disappear, then he wants to uncover who killed his dad, then he challenges his girlfriend Ophelia to tell the truth, then he helps stage a play to get his suspect Claudius in the open, and then he fights a duel with Laertes over the death of Ophelia and honor. In elevating the style of the well-worn revenge play, Shakespeare created a new theatrical character with his Hamlet, a man who, while conventionally avenging his father's murder, goes deeper, not simply into retaliatory actions but also into himself, his nature, his thoughts.

Tom Joad's journey in *The Grapes of Wrath* occurs in the context of his traveling with his dispossessed family across Depression era America. Recently released from jail and under the restrictions of his parole, he confronts the predatory injustice of individuals and the system that fractures his family. In order to get cheap labor from distressed midwestern farmers, corporate managers have distributed misleading flyers that advertise plentiful jobs in California. This charade has set off a worker stampede for a livelihood out West that doesn't exist. Frank Galati's adaptation focuses on Tom's through-line to hold the theatrical event together. Tom's inner moral struggles play out during his clashes with the socioeconomic forces thwarting the dispossessed Okies, and they sustain the primary conflict of his attempts to create a more just society.

Other Examples of Play Conflicts

- *King Lear:* Lear wants a show of total love; his daughters want respect or power.
- *Romeo and Juliet:* They want an idealized love to stop the families' war.
- *Enough:* A wife overcomes her lack of a self in order to be able to leave.
- *Me and My Shadow/*"Petition": Brothers of opposite temperaments fight to overpower one another.
- *The Cockfighter:* The parents want to shape their son's destiny; he wants his own.

Finding the Central Event

Central events are actions, turning points in the lives of characters that change them. Once a character declares something of significance or

Fig. 6. *The Cockfighter.* Sonny bonding with the prize bird, Lion. (Danny Seckel, Actors Theater of Louisville, 1999.)

does a crucial deed, those actions dramatically alter how the characters interact. To help find the storyline, focus on what you feel is the most important character and his or her central event. You took a pass at finding this moment when you were choosing material and naming your theme. This is your chance to check your choice and hone your language in naming it. Often the central event is comparable to the Aristotelian climax: the major event that occurs as the plot complications build to a rising action.

Example of the Central Event of a Play

Although the most dramatic event in *The Cockfighter* is the championship match that Sonny loses, it is not the central event of the story or the adaptation. The central event happens later in the play in the moments of recognition that had struck me in my earliest readings of the novel, as I described in chapter 2 on dialogue and narrative:

MOTHER: You said it wasn't Sonny's fault.

FATHER: It was, and it wasn't. I thought he couldn't lose with that cock, and he did.

MOTHER: You said it had some kind of disease.

FATHER: One thing I hate is that he didn't tell me. He just threw that cock away.

MOTHER: I don't see how he could have known.

FATHER: I'd have known. If it was me, I would have told.

MOTHER: That's silly, Jake. You don't know what you'd do if you were him.

FATHER: I'd have taken an interest in it. You know me. I'd do it like I do right now. I always have, and I always will.

MOTHER: I know that, Jake.

FATHER: I'm not like him. Never have been and never will be.

(Shift.)

BOY: As soon as he said that, I knew what it was. The last piece snapped into place. I wasn't him and never would be, and not only that, I never would want to. Each one was different. That was the puzzle. (151; see also the novel, 197)

The central event occurs when the father, who has won control of the boy, sees him as a loser and cuts him loose, freeing the boy to be himself.

If you identify the central event for your principal character, defined by your theme, you have the essential elements of the story. Your theme is the idea, the impetus that drives your story. The central event is the actual physical action that reveals the decisive turning point around that idea.

From "This is a story of a man who could not make up his mind," we can deduce that Hamlet is the principal character and his greatest moment of oscillation—when he doesn't kill Claudius at prayer—is the central event of the storyline Olivier has stated. If adaptor Frank Galati thought the storyline of *The Grapes of Wrath* was "Americans' loss of faith as hard times hit," he would have selected more material for ex-preacher Casy. Instead, *The Grapes of Wrath* adaptation storyline focuses on the Joad family and the central event of arriving in the Promised Land.

- The "Petition" story is about the Siamese twin brothers, and the central event is the front brother's decision to separate from the back brother.
- In "Enough," the woman is the principal character, and her central event is the step she takes to leave.

• *A Christmas Carol* is the story of Scrooge's redemption. The central event is his breakup with Belle.

You can identify the central event not just of the whole story but also of each scene. A central event is an action, physical or vocal, that demonstrably changes the relationship or the character in a scene. When Cordelia refuses to play the "commodification of love" game with King Lear, the world they live in falls apart. When Scrooge ignores his fiancée Belle as his greed overcomes him, the relationship is shattered. A good scene builds up to this central event, the moment of no going back. The aftermath gives the characters new obstacles to overcome.

Example of a Central Event in The Grapes of Wrath

One central event of a scene, early on in *The Grapes of Wrath,* involves the recognition moment of a father being able to see his son released from incarceration.

> PA: What do you want? (His hammer is suspended in the air. He turns and looks at Tom. The hammer drops slowly to his side.) It's Tommy. It's Tommy come home. (16)

The hammer slowly dropping is a lovely central event action, revealing Pa's diligent need to work and the soft shock of seeing his long-absent son returned from prison.

The major central event for both the novel and the script adaptation of *The Grapes of Wrath* happens when Tom Joad, held in check by his parole throughout the story, vents his pent-up rage and deep sense of justice by avenging his preacher friend's killing at the hands of the henchman sent to drive them away. This action will break the Joad family apart.

Most plays build to a major central event with smaller, scene-by-scene central events. This is a useful shaping idea. Playwrights build dramatic tension within the scenes and then interconnect the chain of scenes to the longer storyline and theme.

One of the key scenes of *The Cockfighter* is the cockfight itself. The novel and play's title give us the story's focus—the boy handling the birds—while the plot moves inexorably toward the champion match.

Here the sly, proud father pushes the trusting son into the center ring to get the odds in his favor, since he believes his champion bird can't lose, and also as a rite of passage into manhood for his son. As I described and illustrated with the excerpt in chapter 2, on dialogue and narration, the father viciously barks the narration (excerpted in chapter 2, on dialogue and narration) simultaneously against the mother's awed voice. The audience watches Sonny center stage, his body lacerated through empathy as the fight mangles his favorite pet.

Prior Circumstances: The Past That Shapes the Future

Crucial facts from the past that shape the present are prior circumstances, and your task is to identify which are indispensable for your audience to know. This part of the building block is like an archaeological dig to find information that affects the characters' current playable choices, options, and habits. Prior circumstances are major events that occurred before the present action of the play. These events are often revealed in exposition (dialogue between characters that is designed to fill us in on these facts) or soliloquy.

That the sins of the father are visited on the son is the dramatic reality of Ibsen's play *Ghosts*. As the play progresses, it reveals the past and makes it present, both in the plot and in the acting. Oswald the son had a dissolute, syphilitic father whose death left him with an inheritance both economic and biological. Oswald's mother covered up her husband's past of indiscretions, temporarily restoring his reputation. Although the father never appears in the play, his specter, revealed through exposition and confession, shrouds the play's atmosphere as Oswald pushes for the light of truth while his brain disintegrates. Ibsen's careful release of the prior circumstances of the father's true nature heightens the stakes for the characters as the play progresses.

In some stories, very little of the past impinges on the narrative in the novel or the revealed actions of the play. In other stories, there is plenty of crucial information that needs to be made clear, but the adaptor does not have to dramatize all the months when drought created the Dust Bowl in Oklahoma, farms were foreclosed and families left the scorched land. The information can be acted in silence, narrated, or delivered in dialogue form.

Example from The Grapes of Wrath: *Evoking the Drought and Prison*

The first five pages of *The Grapes of Wrath* novel describe the dusty, scarred earth that decimated the Joads' farm. This is the overwhelming, defining prior circumstance of these characters' lives before the action of the story begins. A one-paragraph monologue opens the stage adaptation and evokes this prior circumstance.

> FIRST NARRATOR: The dawn came, but no day. (*Particles of dust hang in the air as feeble light spreads up into the sky.*) In the morning the dust hung like fog. Men stood by their fences and looked at the ruined corn, drying fast now, only a little green showing through the film of dust. And the women came out of the houses to stand beside their men—to feel whether this time the men would break. The women studied the men's faces secretly. For the corn could go as long as something else remained. (9)

Chapter 2 in the novel teases out Tom Joad's disclosure of his incarceration in McAlester Prison to a truck driver he has manipulated into giving him a ride. In the compressed time and space of the stage version, the meeting of Tom and Preacher Casy, two of the central characters, reveals this crucial prior circumstance:

> TOM: Guess I'll mosey along.
> CASY: It's a funny thing. I was thinkin' about ol' Tom Joad when you came along. Thinkin' I'd call on him. How is Tom?
> TOM: I don't know how he is. I ain't been home in four years.
> CASY: Been out travelin' around?
> TOM: (*suspiciously*) Didn't you hear about me? I was in the papers.
> CASY: No, I never. What?
> TOM: I been in McAlester them four years.
> CASY: Ain't wantin' to talk about it, huh? I won't ask you no more questions, if you done something bad—
> TOM: I'd do what I done again. I killed a guy. In a fight. We was drunk at a dance. He got a knife in me, an' I killed him with a shovel that was layin' there. Knocked his head plumb to squash.
> CASY: You ain't ashamed of nothin' then?
> TOM: No, I ain't. I got seven years account of he had a knife in me. Got out in four—parole. (10)

Most of the dialogue is verbatim, culled from approximately ten pages of chapter 4 in the novel. Adaptor Galati inserted a slightly forced transition when preacher Casy says to young Tom Joad, "It's a funny thing. I was thinkin' about ol' Tom Joad when you came along" as an expedient way to connect their travels (12).

Example: Unearthing the Past in The Cockfighter

In *The Cockfighter,* there are lovely patches of narrative that describe the vitality and glamour of the father when he was a popular, athletic high school student. His demanding, archetypal male behavior in the adaptation gains a softer edge by including this prior circumstance information. A consistent mistake in adapting for the stage is attempting to pull too much expository information into the living reality of a play from the more reflective, purely verbal form of the novel. An actor capable of suggesting the athletic past of the father can splice a few appropriate sports actions onto lines of the text. Such playable actions can bring the prior circumstances of the characters into present time. Knowing that the description would overburden the narrative drive of the play, I also chose to include some of the father's charming and playful aspects during moments with his son. One strategy involved including the following joke, which they share in the midst of the mother's distress when her husband looks like he is dressed to go fighting:

> FATHER: Damn right. You don't get dressed up to go to a cockfight unless you're Benny Easley, maybe.
> BOY: Benny Easley's the county commissioner and the only man ever known to go to a cockfight dressed up in a suit and tie. He always said he had an appointment later on.
> FATHER: An appointment with an undertaker, they said. Haw! Haw! (123)

The boy is in on the joke with his dad, mocking someone of higher stature to feel better about themselves.

The Beginning, Middle, and End of a Clear Storyline

Now that you know your conflicts, central events, and prior circumstances, you're well prepared to revisit your single-sentence statement of storyline.

Examples of Storylines

- "Petition": The demure back brother of Siamese twins supplicates to be separated from the front brother after they both fall for a contortionist.
- "Enough": A woman leaves her husband.
- *A Christmas Carol:* Scrooge faces his past and future to become a better man.
- *The Grapes of Wrath:* The Joads survive seemingly insurmountable catastrophes and create a newly bonded and redefined family.
- *The Cockfighter:* A boy nurtures a pet and then is driven to destroy it.

A strong storyline engages the audience in the forward movement of the theater experience, the "then, and then, and then," as the actions of the characters enlighten, disturb, and move us. What drives the moving train of central events through your adaptation is plot, fueled by conflict. Each compartment, whether a scene or monologue, should have a definable event that moves the story forward.

The front cars of the train, the early events, are actions that incite the conflict. This is the beginning of the story. Here the adaptor gets the audience to care about a character, relationship, or theme. In the middle of the ride, certain events develop and complicate the conflict, forcing the characters, and us, to take sides. The concluding events resolve the conflict. They help the audience see what has changed. These can be external, social actions, such as Tom Joad's declaring that he will stand up for the kind of justice that the unfortunate Casy believed in, or internal, such as the self-reflective recognition that clarifies a life path for Jake's rejected boy Sonny.

Finding an ending for their stories daunts most writers. In an adaptation this task is less complicated, since you are working from a text that has an ending already. If your adaptation boldly alters the focus from that of the original by focusing on a secondary or singular character, theme, or storyline, you assume more responsibility for selecting and arranging the text to build to your desired culmination. In any case, the trick is building to the central event of your play by choosing the right material to lead the audience to the emotional and intellectual conclusion you want. Your statement of storyline guides you through the overall arc of the journey. The theme gives it substance and the conflicted human dimension.

✦ ✦ ✦ ✦

CONSTRUCTION EXERCISES FOR BUILDING BLOCK 5

For Conflict

In chapter 3, on character and relationship, you touched on what some of the pivotal conflicts are between your characters or within a given character. Now it's time to apply what you've learned in building block 5 to identify those with certainty.

A. Using your previous notes on character, remember the needs of the principal characters. Note the obstacles that thwart them in meeting those needs.

B. To define a conflict, figure out something your character wants that he or she is not getting. What is most important to the character, the struggle that drives his or her actions for the full arc of the story? In a pivotal relationship between two characters, decide what each needs from the other but isn't getting.

C. For each two characters, find five major actions that change their journeys. Spread your choices throughout the material to uncover the arc the writer built to reveal his or her story. Refer back to your answers to questions about character from building block 3 and figure out which of the major actions you noted are key moments of the characters facing their conflict.

For Central Events

Read the scenes from the latest draft of the rough-cut script you started building in chapter 2, plus any other scenes you may have added after studying character and relationship in chapter 3 and image in chapter 4.

D. What is your most important scene in the play? Remember your theme to help you make this choice if you're unsure. In this scene, what is the struggle between your principal character and another? State what happens as simply as you can, in terms of the conflict: what the major character wants versus what another wants that opposes it. What is the *action,* the thing that happens?

E. Look at the central event for each scene you have chosen, including any monologues. Note the actions or lines of dialogue that reveal a moment when something happens that changes the character or relationship. Look for an action or two in each scene that best reveals the story. It is usually a moment when the conflict comes to a head, when a character says or does something that changes a fact about them or changes their own or others' perception of them.

The change can be internal, such as Hamlet's seeing that he is impotent and wishing that this "too solid flesh would melt." But external actions, such as Cordelia's refusing to play the love game with her dad, Lear, are often more dynamic.

F. Work through your text, scene by scene, and look for the central events. For each place you can define a central event, name it with an active verb. The character or relationship does what? What happens?

- Pa Joad drops the hammer.
- The cockfight lacerates Sonny's body.
- The father Jake erases his connection to Sonny.

G. Compile these active-verb central events into a list that moves sequentially through the whole play. Rename or reframe them a bit if you need to, in order to link them together. You are building the through-line that will carry your story. Each central event adds weight and dramatic tension to the buildup of the action that best reveals the principal characters and the obstacles they try to overcome. What pattern or forward movement do you see toward the event that you consider most revealing of the story? What obstacles does the principal character face and overcome until failing or winning?

H. Decide which of these moments, these central events, best reveal your story. Answer these questions to check your choices.

- Are there any scenes you chose earlier that now seem less essential and could be cut?
- Are key events missing from the arc of the story?
- Is your central character pivotal in the scenes you've selected, or are those scenes possibly pointing toward a different choice of central character?
- What storyline do these linked events suggest?
- You know from your work on conflict what the clashes are, between or within characters. Is there sufficient material in your chosen scenes to escalate, advance, or resolve the conflict?

For Prior Circumstance

Now that your sequence of events is taking shape in your evolving cut-and-paste draft, you can check to see whether your audience knows what they need to know for the story to make sense.

I. Return to your source material and highlight in a new color all references to events that happened in the past. Decide what essential information your audience needs to know about your characters in order to understand what is happening in the present action of the play.

J. Of these essential aspects of the past, assign as many as possible to be played out in elements other than direct expository dialogue: the environment (dust in the hot lights for drought in *The Grapes of Wrath*), character (the father joke in *Cockfighter*), relationship (Casy and Tom's penitentiary revelation), or conflict (mom-dad tension over Sonny reaching puberty).

K. If you find prior circumstances that can't be dramatically embedded in the present, look for moments when characters can deliver this information and decide where to embed it in dialogue or narrative monologue.

For Stating Your Storyline

Your achievement in this building block will be in knowing what story you want to tell. Using what you know about your theme, who your central characters are, the main conflict, and the central events you've outlined, can you now focus enough to define your storyline, if you haven't already?

L. State the story in one simple, declarative sentence. Say it out loud or write it down. Phrase it as you would to a third-grade class.

M. To test your statement of storyline and revise it if you need to, answer these questions for yourself.
   - Does it still feel weighty and worth working on?
   - Will this story fit with your theme?
   - Does it include your main character?
   - Does it give your adaptation the broad arc that will sustain the drive of the story all the way to its end?
   - Does it suggest or point toward the major event that you have chosen as central?

N. Tell your storyline statement to a peer. Without any further leading or prompting from you, ask what that person finds engaging, moving, or relevant in it. Does it intrigue him or her?

O. Using the scene-by-scene list of central events you've written (for exercise F), tell your friend the story of your play in this brief outline form. Does it capture your listener's interest? Is it confusing? If you have identified the central event of the whole story well, it will be the climactic moment that you are most excited about revealing.

P. Test your outline in light of storyline:

- Do your principal characters fail or succeed with their obstacles, their relationships, and their own natures substantively enough for you to feel the journey is worth it?
- Does your sequence of central events include a beginning, middle, and end in the sense that you learned about in this chapter?

Q. Write at least one scene that caught your attention during your work on storyline in this chapter. Choose a scene that you need to clarify for exploration of the conflict, to fill in prior circumstance, or because it is the most important scene in the play.

I hope that knowing clearly what story you want to tell has given you new excitement for telling it and momentum to carry you through to a finished script. Having (1) articulated what it was that first captured you about your material thematically, (2) learned how to adapt narrative into dialogue, (3) decided which characters feel right to share the story onstage, and (4) chosen an evocative stageable image to help guide your choices, you should now have (5) a framework on which to hang the rest of your work as an adaptor. You now know where to lay your building blocks. Next we will check to make sure that your play is truly stageworthy by ensuring that it includes playable action.

6 ✦ *Building Block Six*

Craft Playable Actions

Theater is doing. It lives and moves in real time, and things have to happen during that time for your play to be theater. Earlier chapters have touched on the need for actions in your script, and chapter 5 in particular explored the necessity of adding action to storyline. An action is what happens, the actual physical occurrence that defines the central event of a scene or your play. A series of such actions carries your story forward. This chapter will focus on defining an action and pointing you toward crafting a script that relies on this essential theatrical element.

Just as all the building blocks work together, intersect, and feed one another, the three performance vocabularies of language, image, and movement actually overlap and support each other in their work of communicating meaning. Language conveys an action when it is revelatory, when, at that present moment of speaking, it uncovers what someone wants. Playable events involving costumes, props, lights, sound, and the scenic environment allow an evocative stageable image to effect an action. And actors' physical or vocal playing choices that reveal their internal changes of emotion or shifts in their relationships are pure, straightforward theatrical actions.

Language as Action

In life we use a lot of words, sounds, stock phrases, and tangled eloquence before we get to the point. In contrast, the best words onstage have an economy and direct specificity. Such language is action when the words a character speaks change the course of the story. Often such a linguistic action takes us by surprise or, conversely, answers a question to which everyone has been waiting for an answer. When someone announces his or her candidacy for mayor or withdraws from the race, either is an action. When a child says, "I'm running away," or a friend tells a lie to spread a rumor, each is an action. When someone says "I love you" for the first time, or "I don't love you anymore," delivering this news is an action. It changes the behavior of the characters in the scene. Many of the significant events we encounter as human beings we experience through language—it is the medium through which we receive many of the gifts, blows, discoveries, and challenges that life has to offer. So scenes onstage reflect this language-mediated human experience, and great actors are beautifully adept at making these moments of action clear. The physical and vocal buildup to both delivering and receiving these central-event lines between actors makes them the powerful moments that we remember from a play.

One of the clearest examples of spoken language as a character's action is a vow. When someone commits with certainty to a significant course of action that he or she has been considering, it is the utterance of that fact that makes it real and communicates it both to any other characters onstage and to the audience. Sometimes it is news to the character as well.

Example of Language as Action from Hamlet

Brooding, grief-bound, "melting" Hamlet turns into a man of moves after he discovers that his father was murdered.

> GHOST: If thou didst ever thy dear father love—
> HAMLET: O God!
> GHOST: Revenge his foul and most unnatural murder.
> HAMLET: Murder!
> GHOST: Murder most foul, as in best it is, but this most foul, strange, and unnatural.
> HAMLET: Haste me to know't, that I with wings as swift as meditation, or thoughts of love, may sweep to my revenge. (I, V)

Hamlet answers the demand of his dead, militaristic father with the linguistic action of pledging, in the final line of this passage, to avenge his father's murder. At this moment, vengeance becomes his superobjective for the play, and all his actions follow this need.

Example of Language as Action from The Cockfighter

A significant action in *The Cockfighter* is Sonny's exclaiming, "Fight it out!" He puts his beloved and wounded pet Lion back in the ring to fight to the death. The buildup to Sonny's choice occurs as Homer tries to concede the fight and save Lion for the boy, while the father counts off and insists that it is in the nature of a cock to kill or be killed.

> FATHER: (*Coming up.*) What's going on here? What? Hell, no! Fight it out. I don't give up.
> HOMER: That's you. That ain't that chicken. Why not let the boy have it?
> FATHER: Hell, no! White-headed son of a bitch. Get on with it.
> HOMER: (*To the boy*) That's what you want to do?
> FATHER: What the hell you asking him for? I'm the owner. I already told you. (*Starts the count.*) One, two . . .
> HOMER: He's the handler of record.
> FATHER: (*To the boy*) Three, four . . .
> HOMER: How about it?
> FATHER: Five, six . . .
> HOMER: Keep it. Don't let them kill him.
> FATHER: Seven, eight . . .
> HOMER: You got a dog?
> (*Boy shakes his head no.*)
> HOMER: Go on and keep it, then. Chickens make good pets. Follow you around wherever you go, if you let them.
> FATHER: Nine, ten.
> BOY: Fight it out!
> FATHER: PIT THEM! (144)

The father never wavers from his insistence that the cock fight to the death, as he reinforces with his shouted rejoinder. But the boy's "Fight it out!" signifies a crucial decision on his part: to go along, to cooperate, and to let his bird be killed in the unfair fight.

Plays are filled with language, and though all of it relates to what the character wants, only some of it enacts a specific action. And though, of course, speaking involves an actor's physically doing something— moving lips and making sounds—not every utterance changes the course of the story at that moment. Though in a carefully crafted piece there is always some reason for the words to be included, there are other reasons besides immediately turning the tide of the story. Language delivers expository information that lays groundwork for future moments of action, language establishes character or relationship, language voices reflections, and language paints an image. But do remember, when you are looking for the central action of a scene, that it can and often does occur in the words, and this is language's most theatrical use.

Image as Action

The evocative stageable image and other aspects of the design can also be expressive vehicles of action in a play. It is rare, but it does sometimes happen that a design element participates in creating key events in a scene. For instance, if you have chosen a bright, searing, focused light as the central image for your adaptation, then this performance vocabulary becomes meaningful in a production of your play. Whenever this light appears, it carries a certain weight and meaning within the context of your story, something your audience can quickly learn to understand. If you've written your adaptation so that your characters are also aware of this light, then your actors can react to it—even a refusal to react to it takes on meaning. In this context, the appearance of that particular kind of light is an action. In Beckett's *Play,* for example, spotlights force three adulterous characters, stuck in urns, to speak their truth.

Of the three performance vocabularies, image is the one least often used to communicate an action. The visual world shapes the audience's experience of the play powerfully, but it doesn't tend to intervene and drive a major change in the action; it takes big-budget pyrotechnics to create and re-create every night a wall falling down or an onstage storm. The two design elements most practical to employ within scenes as actions, as events that change the direction of the characters' choices, are light (as in the previous examples) and sound. In Kushner's *Homebody/Kabul,* the sound cue of the Islamic call to prayer forces the Arab character to stop and pray toward Mecca while the English girl responds emotionally to the haunting chant.

Example of Light Imagery as Action in The Cockfighter

In *The Cockfighter,* beads of light evoke eyes staring out of the dark in both the novel and the play, so light becomes a key image in the stage design. During one scene in our production, Sonny held a bright silver cage over his head. He was looking at his beloved pet Lion. The cage, rigged with tiny strip lights operated by radio waves, grew bright as the parents intoned the voice-over narrative, up until "the ancient eye looked out." Then, fading until the mother's word "vacancy" at the end of her line, the cage became black.

> MOTHER: It was a secret. He felt the cage tremble when Lion shifted. The head rotated, and its ancient eye looked out. The eye was so dark there was no light reflected in it. It looked like a hole or vacancy.
> FATHER: Then it blinked. (120–21)

On the word "blinked," the light flashed, creating a visual analogue to the blinking warrior Lion—its mystery and its dark eye evoked by the lighting design.

As with language, there are many uses of image that are not actions. No matter how richly layered with meaning, the images in your play are only context, environment, and props unless you incorporate them into the story. A twelve-foot abstract statue in the middle of your set may be your evocative stageable image, pregnant with metaphor, but it is not an action. Your main character's hitting it, hugging it, or moving it can be a significant action. Having it fall and break the character's leg is an action. Similarly, technical effects to evoke a thunderstorm might cast the right mood for a scene, but the weather is not an action unless it somehow changes the course of things, for example, keeping everyone from going on the big picnic or prompting two shy lovers to shed their clothes on a hot deserted beach.

One notable convergence of image, language, and action occurs when a significant action happens in an image but is impractical to create literally onstage, so that the playwright uses language to narrate the imagistic event that changes the course of the action. We see its effects but not necessarily the moments when their impact occurs. For instance, the storm in *King Lear* is a decisive event in the plot, driving Lear to see, for the first time, the destitution of the poor in his kingdom. Rather than ask a theater company to create an unconvincing storm of rain and thunder onstage, Shakespeare lets his characters narrate this event in imagery for the audience. Another example of a language-invoked central image is in the title of Chekhov's *The Cherry Orchard*. Although, according to Chekhov's script, the audience never sees the cherry orchard literally represented onstage in the play, the descriptions of it by various characters conjure for the audience their own images of beautiful, pastoral

Edens of untouched nature. At the end of the play, Chekhov employs the aural effect of chopping sounds as the orchard is cut down.

Physical Action as a Direct Theatrical Vocabulary

And then there is the simple, clear action of a character physically doing something. When this something is essential to the scene, changes the course of events, or reveals something of note, it is an essential action that you need to write into your script. Finding a physical life for characters that supports the script's spoken words is the work of actors, and staging their physical interactions with other actors and in the environment is the director's job. If you have great collaborators, they will find all sorts of nuances, quirks, physical habits, and activities for your characters that you never dreamed of. You can feed their work by looking for what you know about the characters and building a few well-suited actions into some of their scenes.

For instance, when Galati adapted the scene between Ma Joad and Rose of Sharon in which Ma chides Rose for crying and orders her to make herself useful, Galati included the action of peeling potatoes as an integral part of the scene. Knowing Ma Joad's industrious practicality, it would have made little sense to have the two of them simply sitting for that conversation, and the work at hand gave Ma something specific to exhort Rose to do instead of crying (60–61).

Don't confuse a mere activity with an essential action. An activity is something physical that actors do to accompany a scene, something that works with the dialogue in the scene and fits with their character choices but could be replaced with a different activity and have the scene still make sense. In a given scene, a grandfather talking to various family members in the kitchen could be cooking breakfast, reading the paper, or polishing silver; each would offer a distinct interpretation of the character, and any of them might work. You don't need to make all those scene-by-scene activity choices and write them into the script; leave this work to able actors and directors.

An action goes beyond an activity by becoming essential and therefore integral. The actions to find for your scenes are important, defining, nonverbal physicalizations that change the course of the story. Including such key physical actions not only gives your collaborators important character information but also gives you an opportunity to rely on this distinct other performance vocabulary, this specifically theatrical one.

Some actions are better for your actors to play than for any of them to narrate. These you can write into stage directions. While I included much of the narrative material from the *Cockfighter* novel in the play by assigning it to characters, I also took many of the narrated physical actions from the novel and brought them directly into the production for the actors to play. Since I was directing the adaptation, as well as writing it, I was able to envision and include many such physical actions for the piece, whether or not I wrote them in the stage directions.

For instance, in the novel, narrative describes Sonny nurturing his pet chicken. He cradles it, gives it the nickname Lion, strokes its feathers, and cares for its grooming and eating. In the play I could dispense with stating these actions and have the actor selectively play the physical choices that reveal his adolescent playfulness and sense of camaraderie with a favorite pet. Look for these evocative physical actions in your source. Particularly if you are not going to be involved in the rehearsal process for your script, write the most revelatory ones into stage directions to feed the theater artists who will collaborate to produce it.

Example of Telling Physical Actions from The Cockfighter

After failing to cajole Sonny to eat breakfast, his mother runs to the departing truck to force a peanut butter and jelly sandwich on him. The stage direction reads, "*Mother tries to open the door of the truck*" (128). The father responds to her efforts by renewing their ongoing argument over raising Sonny. The father drives the truck away as she futilely chases after it, and Sonny simultaneously narrates her physical action.

> BOY: She was still running along beside the truck, trying to keep up. All I had to do was turn my head, and there she was. I hated to see her. She was too crazy looking. We picked up speed, and then she was gone. I didn't even turn around to see where she was for fear I'd turn into a pillar of salt like it says in the Bible. I kept my eyes straight ahead—it wasn't just a whole new day. It was a whole new life. There was no telling where we were going or what we were going to do when we got there.

Finally, farther down the road, Sonny aligns with Dad and rebels against Mom, signaling this alliance with the pivotal physical action of the scene, as described in the stage direction: "*He suddenly rolls down the windows and throws out the peanut butter and jelly sandwich*" (128–29).

The clear dramatic moments that pure physicality creates are sometimes particularly effective in climactic moments near the end of a play. Beckett's "Enough" occurs in the mind of the older wife who imagines a life away from her sick husband. In my adaptation she literally took the steps that also represented her monumental inner movement forward. At the end of Ibsen's *A Doll's House*, Nora slams the door. This act is particularly theatrical since her husband spends the moments after she leaves the room hoping that she will return. Slamming the door, which the audience hears but doesn't see, is a decisive action that changes the end of the play. She shuts the door on her family, her children, and her former life. Such an actor-driven event utilizes the unique vocabulary of performance—physical action—that another medium, such as a painting or a novel, lacks. Look for opportunities to incorporate such moments of pure performance into your script.

Example of a Physical Action from the Final Moments of The Grapes of Wrath

Steinbeck offers a poetic testament to the humanity of the Joads, and Galati chose this scene to end his script. Rose gives a healing gift to the starving father of a distraught boy: her unused breast milk.

> BOY: He's dyin', I tell you! He's starvin' to death, I tell you.
>
> MA: Hush. (*Ma looks at Pa and Uncle John. She turns to Rose of Sharon now wrapped in the comfort. The two women look at each other. The girl's eyes widen.*)
>
> ROSE OF SHARON: Yes.
>
> MA: I knowed you would. I knowed!
>
> ROSE OF SHARON: (*Whispering.*) Will—will you all go out? (*Ma brushes the hair from her daughter's eyes and kisses her on the forehead.*)
>
> MA: Come on, you fellas. You come out in the shed. (*The boy opens his mouth to speak.*) Hush. Hush and git. (*Ma helps the boy up and leads him to the open door. Uncle John, Pa and the children leave. The boy looks back after his father and then goes out. Ma stands in the door for a few moments, looking back at Rose of Sharon, and then goes. Rose of Sharon stands still in the whispering barn. Then she draws the comfort about her and moves slowly to the man and stands looking down at the wasted face, into the wide frightened eyes. She slowly kneels down beside him, loosens one side of the blanket and bares her breast. He shakes his head feebly from side to side.*)

ROSE OF SHARON: You got to. (*She bends low. Her hand moves behind his head and pulls him up gently.*) There. (*Her eyes gleam.*) There. (*A violin plays in the distance. As the lights fade slowly, Rose of Sharon looks up and across the barn. Her lips come together and smile mysteriously.*) (87)

The added information about Rose's "mysterious smile" conjures archetypal images of nurturing, mothering, and the Christ-like action of giving her body for one in need. This physical action of giving her body and pulling the man to a pieta-like position while shrouding him in her blanket, the trenchant text that accompanies the action, and the solitude of the empty barn combine to blend movement, language, and image into a powerful, dynamic interweaving of mutually reinforcing actions. The stage direction's suggestion of a distant violin also supports the bittersweet tone of the scene as conceived for the stage.

Example of Multilayering Performance Vocabularies from Macbeth

The following active interplay of actions in *Macbeth,* combining props, movement, and the imagery of blood also reveals great theatrical writing of actions:

LADY MACBETH: Go get some water, and wash this filthy witness from your hand. Why did you bring these daggers from the place? They must lie there. Go carry them, and smear the sleepy grooms with blood.

MACBETH: I'll go no more. I am afraid to think what I've done; look on't again I dare not.

LADY MACBETH: Infirm of purpose! Give me the daggers.

Taking the dripping daggers in her hands seals Lady Macbeth's fate. Burning the blood into her hands leads to her constant attempts to clean her hands, her futile "out, out damn spot," and finally her suicide.

Effective Stage Directions for Essential Actions

"*Exit pursued by a bear.*" This famous stage direction from *The Winter's Tale* is an exception to the notable sparseness of explicit stage directions in surviving editions of Shakespeare's plays. And while portraying a live bear may be a challenge to the design team, certainly this event is an action pivotal to the plot, since it drives Antigonus away and leaves the baby Perdita to be discovered and reared by the Shepherd.

Playwrights vary wildly with the amount of stage direction they insert into a script to clue readers, producers, directors, actors, and designers as to what is happening and how to envision it. George Bernard Shaw wrote voluminous stage directions, often much longer than the dialogue, while Wole Soyinka leaves it to his collaborators' imaginations to discover the actions, attitude, and look of a scene through an engagement with words he has written for the actors to speak.

The text of your original material is a rich source of references that reveal what motivates the characters. How much explanation you pull into the script testifies to both your skill and your personal style as an adaptor: enough so that the collaborators can sense what to play, but not so much that it overwhelms the script with details so sticky that the spoken text becomes impossible to play in the way you describe it. One trap is the temptation to write into stage directions the emotional results you expect the actors to play. When these appear in published scripts, they are often not clues written by the playwright but obvious possible attitude choices inserted by the editor to help the reading public follow the scene.

My own guide is to put in only stage directions that are needed to make a crucial action clear, that tap the performance vocabulary of playable actions essential to the progress of a scene. If you choose to follow this guide, the way to test whether to leave a stage direction in or take it out is to try omitting it and see if the subsequent lines and the rest of the scene still make sense. If the stage direction says that one character whacks another over the head with a crowbar and renders him unconscious, the scene can't proceed without the actors knowing that essential action.

Examples from The Grapes of Wrath *of Effective Stage Directions*

The following stage directions are clues to playing a brutal prior circumstance. Ma Joad has held her dead mother all night so they could get to a safe place and not be stopped by the agricultural guards at a border crossing. This harrowing experience, which the audience does not see onstage, leads to the following actions.

(Ma stumbles out from behind the truck.)
TOM: My god, Ma, you sick?
MA: You say we're acrost? *(Her face is putty-like. She holds on to the truck.)*
TOM: Look! *(She turns her head. Her mouth opens a little and her fingers go to her throat and gather a little pinch of skin.)*
TOM: You sick, Ma?
MA: No jus' tar'd.
TOM: Was Granma bad?
MA: Granma's dead. (47)

And in the following example, Galati offers revealing clues to the actor playing Ma Joad about characterization, her stalwart nature, and letting go of her beloved son.

TOM: Now I better go.
MA: Goodbye. *(Ma takes his head in her hands and kisses him on the brow. Tom stands up and turns to leave. Ma reaches for him but when Tom turns around she pulls her hand back suddenly.)* (79)

Examples of Physical Action in Stage Directions from The Cockfighter

Here is an example of a stage direction that I culled from the novel. Its function is to suggest one of the broad, animal-inspired gestures that I wanted to encourage the actors to play throughout the stage production. While telling a story about Sonny, the father imitates the boy's distress in swallowing by imitating it in a birdlike movement, and the audience can also enjoy the humor of Dad acting out to entertain his family.

FATHER: One time he was eating too fast. He was always eating too fast, according to her, only this time it was a peanut butter and jelly sandwich, and he couldn't seem to get it down. I said, Do like a dog. Do like this—*(thrusting his neck out two or three times, pretending to swallow it whole)*. (126)

Offering Suggestive Clues in Stage Directions

Besides crucial physical actions, other information that some playwrights include in stage directions can be poetic imagery, character information,

Fig. 7. *Enough.* The girl picks out the stars. (Kirsten Giroux, Theater Works, 1982.)

or detailed descriptions of the set. As you find the amount of stage direction that feels right for your play, remember that since you are adapting from another source, your collaborators have the gift of the original text to which they can return, if that seems useful. There they can discover more about the writer's ideas, the characters' intentions, and possibilities for how and what to play. Also remember that much of the crucial information that will inspire your collaborators nests within the dialogue itself and may not need much embellishment in stage directions to be clear. Even specific physical actions are often implied so clearly in the characters' spoken words, for example, "Put down that knife" or "Let me just finish this slice of pie," that to repeat them in stage directions is unnecessary.

A useful stage direction has something specific to communicate about the character, image, or the events of the story. One scene in *The Cock-fighter* opens with this stage direction: "*Father laughs. Boy joins in, trying to suppress it*" (122). Transitioning through the shift from the previous scene, the father is laughing at the mother. The laughter is an essential action. The boy trying to suppress his laughter is a piece of character information that I included in this stage direction to give an important clue to the boy's changing allegiance between his parents.

Examples of Effective Stage Directions from The Evidence

In his play *The Evidence*, Frank Manley offers this stage direction in a scene that involves a rocking chair: "*From this point on George uses the rocker as part of the rhythm of what he is saying. He uses it like part of his body*" (9). While this stage direction doesn't name an action essential to the scene, it does offer the actor playing George an evocative use of a prop. And in another passage from the same play, Manley integrated this physical action into the dialogue with a stage direction.

> GEORGE: One'd sit there, and the other'd do him.
> LEE: Do what?
> GEORGE: Check them out. Like this. (*He bends* LEE's *head down and goes through his hair, grooming him.*) (38)

The re-creation of a seminal relationship interaction, in this case one creature grooming another, is so outside the experience and imagination of male actors that the playwright's stage direction serves to guide and ground a lovely, testing choice.

Example of Revealing Stage Directions from Ibsen's Enemy of the People

Henrik Ibsen was a master of stage direction. The following example not only vibrantly introduces the protagonist of *An Enemy of the People;* it also states the central theme of the play. Notice how it succinctly employs the set for our eyes to frame Dr. Stockmanns in his front door against the world outside and attunes our ears to his laughter.

> (*She goes to the front door, opens it. Dr. Stockmanns is laughing and talking outside. He is in the prime of his life. He might be called the eternal amateur—a lover of things, of people, of sheer living, a man for whom the days are too short, and the future fabulous with discoverable joys. And for all this most people will not like him—he will not compromise for less than God's own share of the world while they have settled for less than man's.*) (23)

Example of Multiply Evocative Stage Directions from Ibsen's
A Doll's House

In the following excerpt from *A Doll's House,* Nora's subterfuge to control her circumstances is unraveling. Within this one line of dialogue, the playwright interweaves stage directions that treat at least four distinct issues.

- Nora's intense anxiety
- A bell ringing that awakens her to the upcoming negotiation with the contemptible Dr. Rank
- Rank as a character who is hanging an animal in the hall
- The environment growing darker

> NORA: *(Bewildered with terror, stands as though rooted to the ground, and whispers.)* He would do it. Yes, he would do it. He would do it, in spite of all the world.—No, never that, never, never! Anything rather than that! Oh, for some way of escape! What shall I do—! *(Hall bells rings.)* Doctor Rank—!—Anything, anything, rather than—! (NORA *draws her hands over her face, pulls herself together, goes to the door and opens it.* RANK *stands outside hanging up his fur coat. During what follows it begins to grow dark.)* (62)

Example of Suggestive Stage Direction from The Cockfighter

The final stage direction at the end of *The Cockfighter* not only culminates the dramatic buildup of the play but also is a major clue to the style of acting. To make this moment work, the actors need to have tracked throughout the play the rhythms of the boy's silences. His inexpressible change after the death of Lion, his break with his parents, and the savage desecration of his father's prized cocks all build to this vocal moment.

> *(The boy silently roars. His mother and father join in for real. It goes on for a moment, and then almost immediately turns into a general chorus of crowing that sounds like a jubilee. Blackout.)* (154)

I included the idea that this chorus "sounds like a jubilee" in order to capture the idea of the boy's liberation amidst the parents' grief.

Good actors know that they must constantly play evocative, specific choices throughout a play. But if you stopped the play in midperformance and asked, "What is this actor doing right now?" the unfortunate truth is that many are only waiting for the other character to finish so that they can say their next line. This lack of an engaged presence may signify a lazy actor, but often it is also symptomatic of a deeper absence: a script that is only smart chat, lovely language, or self-referential speaking, without clear, playable events. What actors and audiences seek in a script is a production aching with action, with what the characters want, desire, demand, and give in to, with achievable, playable actions that, in life, are often thwarted. Find them. Seed your script with them and give your collaborators and audiences the entrance points into what you found compelling in the story.

✦ ✦ ✦ ✦

CONSTRUCTION EXERCISES FOR BUILDING BLOCK 6

For building block 6, you want to find and utilize urgent, playable actions in your script. This is an opportunity to find the ones you have already included and to write more, or clearer, actions if you find them lacking in your draft.

A. Start by reviewing the best, most recent version of your script. It should have evolved considerably from your first cut-and-paste template in chapter 2 as you worked your way through the building blocks, writing the dialogue and cutting and adding scenes. Look for the central events of the scenes that you defined in chapter 5. Evaluate them one by one to decide which of these key actions occur in the language, which in image or design elements, and which in actors' physical action.

B. Language: Find or write five words, phrases, or sentences that create a perceivable change in the character or the relationship, for example, declarations, taunts, promises, challenges, answers, instigations, pivotal lies, or pivotal truth telling.

C. Image: Find or write three incidents in which the environment activates or enhances a vocal or physical choice by a character. These will most likely appear in stage directions, but dialogue or narrative may refer to them as well.

D. Physical: Find or write five essential and playable tasks or moments for your actors. These can be moments when a character is enticed to act physically or when a character answers a question with a clear nonverbal response. It may be a telling movement, a gesture, or a physical exchange between characters that changes or reveals a relationship. (If you need a refresher on how to do this, refer to the section in chapter 2 on adapting narrative into playable action.)

E. Evaluate your script so far for its use of stage directions. Have you included many? Would your scenes be clearer if you added some stage directions? Would it unburden your script to delete some that you have already included—that is, does your script read more like a novel than a play?

F. Consider the overall style of your piece: what it is about and what mode of action dominates the piece? If you discovered in the exercises that you are relying strongly on image or physical action to communicate with an audience, have you given your collaborators clear stage directions to point them toward ways to make that happen?

G. Review your script to note whether you have embedded a great many stage directions in the dialogue and have included references to various physical actions, design elements, and even attitude choices within the lines that the characters speak. If you choose to leave them in your final script, they should be stage directions that you feel strongly about having enacted in performance.

H. Write clear stage directions to introduce each of your major characters and the set.

The key to success in this building block is to have plenty of clear, playable actions in your script. Whether enacted through language, image, or physicality, these actions should drive your story forward. In particular, the central events that you have chosen for each scene need identifiable moments of action in order to be true central events. If you don't find them in your draft, you now know how to write them in, even if you have to choose some new scenes for your play in order to be sure that something is actually happening.

Part Two

Sturdy Construction: Yours, Mine, & Master Adaptors

7

Balancing the Blocks

There is an intensely delicate balance to the building blocks. Creating three-dimensional characters with complex relationships and vital conflicts in a stageworthy environment takes playmaking choices that resonate with each other while striking that balance. The raw power of live theater allows the paradox of both dynamic immediacy and meditative perspective, and the two combine and combust aesthetically and emotionally when a production achieves a balance of theme, language, character, image, story, and actions.

Different plays give different weights to the content elements, depending on the unique demands of their stories. Some are more weighted and driven by character, such as the back brother in *Me and My Shadow,* or by relationships, such as the Joad clan in *The Grapes of Wrath.* Storyline elements drive some plays, for example, political events and the AIDS epidemic invading the lives of the characters in Tony Kushner's *Angels in America,* or prior circumstance in Ibsen's *Ghosts.* And a few plays structure themselves around a theme, such as transformation in Mary Zimmerman's *Metamorphoses.*

Depending on the needs of the story, the playwright usually finds one performance vocabulary particularly strong for the expressive demands of a piece. Language tends to be a pivotal element in any play, and in some this is especially true. An Oscar Wilde play, such as *The Importance of Being Earnest,* is a luscious illustration of a language-activated piece. Playable physical action is an important building block in theater, and in some plays it is the dominant tool for expression, such as the Molière farce *The Forced Marriage.* Some plays place particular emphasis on incorporating image throughout the script and performance as their animating expressive element, as in *The Cockfighter,* the cockfighting ring shaped my choices about what to keep and what to leave out, as well as how to conceptualize the story's staging.

Success in completing the construction exercises is in being able to compare your first instincts with your subsequent discoveries about these elements. Look at the material you have culled from the text to substantiate each point. You can test it against what you already know from another building block such as theme, principal character, or storyline. There is an interplay between knowing your principal characters and fleshing out their story: what they are like, what they care about, how they sound, who they relate to and how, what conflicts they attempt to overcome, what in the past influences them, and where they live. What you have learned can give you a wide array of materials with which to finish shaping the construction of your adaptation.

As you evaluate your current draft of the script to discern its strongest elements and discover which you might have neglected, you may be surprised at what you find at this stage of the construction process. Stay open to those surprises. If you realize, for instance, that you are onto a powerful stageable image, don't be afraid to let that realization give new direction to your final rewrites of the script.

What Is Your Significant Content Element?

All three building blocks that involve content materials—theme, character and relationship, and storyline—are indispensable to a good play. If you have actors onstage, there is some form of character to follow. And a play is a story in some way or other, even an experimental piece in which the story is less obvious. Theme is inescapable: there is an idea and an interplay between ideas, manifesting somehow in your play. The question worth asking about a play is this: which of these elements is primary in this particular story?

In a character- or relationship-driven story, what propels the series of events forward comes from within the characters, from decisions they make or actions they take. A character has a thought or feeling and acts on it, and those actions are the central events of scenes. The conflict in such a character-driven play is an inner one, while in a relationship-driven play it's between particular characters that we get to know well. The turning points in the story are more about what the characters do than what gets done to them. Human beings struggling within themselves or with other individual human beings, all in ways the audience gets to see and feel, dominate character-oriented stories.

In the character-driven play *Hedda Gabler,* by Henrik Ibsen, the title character is the daughter of a strict military father who has taught her to shoot and ride. She is headstrong and opinionated, yet bound by the nineteenth-century conventions of her sex. The clash of character traits—morbidly self-lacerating, beautiful and aware of it, cold, socially vibrant—leads her to suicide. And Terrence McNally's *Frankie and Johnny in the Clair de Lune* is a relationship-driven play, equally focused on each of the title characters as it traces the progress of their relationship. One night, after only peripheral contact at their jobs in a downscale New York diner, they end up in bed together, unfolding their essential desires, insecurities, and personal histories. The buttons they push in each other unmask ways to accept each other.

In a plot-driven story, a series of events (often unexpected ones) decides what happens next. As audience members we watch the main characters react and deal with these external happenings, which may come from sources that are impersonal or far beyond their influence. The conflict in such plays usually falls in the categories of a human versus society or a human being versus nature. Sometimes such a plot-driven story pits a protagonist against a person about whom so little is known that the antagonist acts more as an impersonal force than a fully developed character.

A particular category of plot-driven story is the one focused on revelations of prior circumstances: the main character tries to find out—or perhaps tries unsuccessfully to avoid finding out—what happened before the action of the play began. Or, in another kind of play about prior circumstances, the discoveries about earlier events keep surprising the characters. The revelations keep changing how they see the world and driving their choices in present relationships.

The storyline of *Oedipus the King* follows the tale of his discovering the awful truth about his past. Mysteries and thrillers are also clear examples of plots driven by revelations of prior circumstances. Polly Teale and England's Shared Experience adapted a notable version of *Jane Eyre.* At the heart of this story lies Jane's stumbling into a series of prior circumstance revelations about her beloved Mr. Rochester's past, in particular that he has locked his mad first wife, Bertha, in the attic. The adaptor makes powerful use of the dramatic form by having this character appear, even before she enters the plot of the play directly, as a ghostlike persona who haunts and reflects Jane. Such a theatrical choice creates the opportunity to explore how past actions dictate present actions, and how Rochester influences Jane.

What Anchors Your Adaptation?

Some plays are evenly balanced between the content elements, though most do tend to tip in a particular direction. In any case, being a character-oriented play doesn't mean that a piece can ignore the need for a good storyline, and a plot moved forward primarily by external events still deserves well-developed characters and relationships. But it will be useful for you to know which kind of play you are adapting so that you can follow through on the unique demands of your piece and don't shortchange your primary content element. Then you can make clear choices about how much to develop its secondary content element.

Theme is the foundation of all other kinds of plays. Whether you are aware of it or not, there is an idea playing itself out in your script. In most plays theme discloses itself primarily through one of the other two types of content: character or storyline. On rarer occasions, often in a piece with a strong conceptual basis or one experimenting with new ways to use performance vocabularies, theme itself will be the dominant content element. We can recognize a play that is likely driven directly by theme and less mediated in its expression by the elements of character or storyline, when the piece does not have a single main character or relationship that it follows closely for the entirety of the play, or when it doesn't have a main, traceable plot over its duration. It may, for instance, have more the feel of a series of vignettes or be highly imagistic. Such a difference from other plays is a clue that it may be a theme-driven play.

If such a piece effectively holds together with a sense of cohesion or unity, then the play is likely following the story of an idea and the play has found a means of tracking that idea and expressing it other than the traditional ones of character or an easily recognizable storyline. I constructed my first significant adaptation, *Of Heaven and Hell,* on a major theme in William Blake's prose, poetry, and graphics: how we process innocence and experience. With no plot and no sustained characters or relationships, I structured the play around the very notion of contrasts: short poems following long; dark pieces that delved into experience following lighter more playful ones that explored innocence; and monologues preceding full-ensemble scenes. And since the script emerged from a collaboration with the ten actors I cast at the beginning of the process, their abilities shaped script choices as well. Who was best suited for which text? Who contrasted visually or vocally with another actor in a way that worked well for the play? The designers and I also allowed the limitations and possibilities of the space, a ballroom with enormous windows, to shape our script choices for this theme-anchored construction.

It's important to step back and take a look at what drives your play at this point in the process because your script may have taken on a life of its own, one that is better than the one you earlier envisioned for it. You may have started your adaptation thinking that you were putting together a deeply moving character study and now find instead that your scenes have revealed an immensely effective plot-driven story. Or you may have planned a traditional-looking story-line piece and find that your material is pushing you into more experimental territory exploring a theme, that your most provocative scenes are unexpected in their emphasis and you'd like to include more of them in that mode.

Sometimes you discover that less is more, as Adrian Hall did in his acclaimed adaptation of *All the King's Men* at Trinity Rep, where on opening day he rearranged and cut forty-five minutes of text to shorten the running time and sharpen the narrative focus.

What Performance Vocabulary Best Serves Your Story?

Each story tends toward its own blend of the three vocabularies of language, image, and physical action. Notice how you use each of these tools. Every play has all three components, except for the rare play in which there are no spoken words whatsoever, which would be particularly surprising in an adaptation from literature—a medium based exclusively on words. And every story tends to utilize one of these modes of communication more than the other two.

In a language-activated play, you notice the words and the writing style. Word choices and syntax take you to a world that is dramatically different from the one you live in, the one you speak in every day. What doesn't work is language that is disconnected from the world it portrays, where the language is self-conscious, noticeable but still not about anything but itself. Such a play sounds written for critics rather than audiences. An effective language-conscious play integrates strong or surprising textual choices with the themes of the story and connects the language style to the content of the events onstage. Plays such as David Mamet's *American*

Buffalo, August Wilson's *Fences,* Suzan-Lori Parks's *Venus,* or Oscar Wilde's *The Importance of Being Earnest* would be significantly less thrilling if you domesticated the finely tuned text. A modern version of *Hamlet* replaces the second line of the play "Stand and unfold yourself" with "Halt, who goes there?" What this dubiously gains in familiar military nomenclature it more than loses in revelatory linguistic imagery by dispensing with the notion of someone—a ghost, as it turns out—"unfolding himself." The language, its reverberations ricocheting in our hearts and minds, is what makes this great play such a profound experience.

An image-oriented play relies strongly on its evocative stageable image and points the adaptor and collaborators toward production choices. If a playwright finds a central image that is powerfully resonant with the original source material, this discovery can start to drive many other choices: which scenes to include, what words to use, stage directions that describe the actors' movements, and both the visual and aural rhythms of the piece. A particularly strong evocative stageable image can even define conclusions about how the story ends, and about the verdict rendered on the theme ideas of the piece. Some plays are indebted to an image or environment choice that sets the characters in an indelible world. Beckett's *Happy Days* has Winnie the wife buried up to her waist in Act One and to her neck in Act Two. The SITI Company (Saratoga International Theater Festival) evoked Orson Welles and *The War of the Worlds* with microphones and constantly shifting frames within frames. In Abi Basch's interracial drama *Voices Underwater,* a new play developed by the Sister City Playwrights Project that premiered concurrently in three cities across the United States, an antebellum house fills with water during the play and the characters respond to and comment on this event in the dialogue.

Most of us have experienced Shakespeare moved from an Elizabethan setting into the Wild West, Nazi Germany, science fiction, a sports arena, the Mafia, and untold other staging metaphors that attempted, and at times succeeded, in finding a resonant frame to help us see the play afresh. Famous examples include Peter Brooks's circus-like *Midsummer Night's Dream* and Beckettesque *King Lear,* Debra Warner's *Richard II* with Fiona Shaw as the feminine king, the Keystone Cops version of *Much Ado About Nothing* at the Public Theater, and Peter Hall's 1920s Venetian-fascist take on *The Merchant of Venice.* Even working with existing, familiar scripts, such radical re-envisionings have sometimes engendered rich new levels of theatricality and meaning for their productions. As an adaptor creating a wholly new theater piece, you can carry the impact of a brave image choice one step further by allowing it to shape your script with language, specific design elements, and the scenes from your original that you decide to omit or include.

Plays that integrate a great deal of essential physical action as a primary means of expression tend to be richly theatrical. Celebrated for reimagining Greek stories and plays in modern settings, Charles Mee wrote *Big Love* with fifty brides in wedding dresses fleeing from their forced marriages in Greece to a villa in Italy. Large physical actions, including the grooms scaling walls and the brides throwing themselves repeatedly to the ground, dominate the staging.

Another play that integrates physical movement in pivotal moments that carry the story forward is *"Master Harold"* . . . *and the Boys* by Athol Fugard. The story, set in apartheid era South Africa, involves two black men working in a small tearoom. Their physical activities of cleaning up, stocking shelves, and waiting on Harold—a young white boy who is the restaurant owner's son—are integral to the events of the play, as is their joyful practicing of their ballroom dancing. And the climactic dramatic event of the play happens in pure physical action, when a fraught verbal exchange culminates in one character baring his backside and the other spitting in his face in response.

Knowing which performance vocabulary your story relies on most gives you a chance to evaluate whether that form is serving your material well. The most important test of whether you have found a performance vocabulary that carries your script is to be sure that your scenes actually have central events. Whether you rely on language, image, or physical action—or, inevitably, some weighted blend of the three—what's important is that there are actions in your play. Things need to happen. Scene after scene of beautiful language won't carry your play if that language doesn't hold key actions in it, such as vows and refusals and decisions and assaults. Similarly, the most striking, thought-provoking set design is only visual art, not theater, if nothing happens in that space. And you can ask your actors to perform stunning feats requiring impressive physical skill, but even if they succeed, your audience won't have a viable evening of theater unless those feats live within the context of a compelling story, action to dramatic action.

Trust Your Hunches

Finding your balance among the elements is a personal process. A successful adaptor continues to take the lead of the original material to

Fig. 8. *Enough.* The wife in her husband's shoes. (Sona Grant, Reality Theater, 1978.)

find that balance all the way through to the final shape of both form and content for the play. When the path seems unclear, return to the personal connection to the material that first captured you. I'm wary of being too prescriptive about these big-picture questions of how to shape your script. It's certainly possible to create a beautiful adaptation for the stage with little conscious attention to the idea of building blocks or balancing content elements and performance vocabularies, even if it is not possible to create a workable piece that actually lacks those elements. Sometimes intuition guides us to artistic choices that we could never have found through a more methodical approach. And certainly I have not consciously followed every step of the processes I outline in this book for every adaptation I have been a part of creating. Most successful adaptations were wrought by artists with significant training and experience in theater or creative writing that helped fortify the instinctual choices of how to construct their adaptation.

But there is an inner logic to a successful play, and within the wide range of approaches that will work to create one there are questions worth asking during the process of that creation, questions that are likely to improve what you offer and make your work more resonant for audiences. Practical questions and evocative questions. My own career is evidence that there is a learnable technique to this work. So by describing many of the approaches and thought processes that I have found useful at one time or another, I am offering you these questions. Asking them is both a way for you to check the writing you have already done that seems to be working well and a crowbar that may get you unstuck when it becomes unclear what step would be most useful next. Continue to listen to your own inner guides, your muse, as you decide which questions will be most helpful to you—especially at this final, big-picture stage of finishing your script—and which you should set aside.

Balancing the Elements

Of the six building blocks, the first, theme, is the beginning and end of your work as an adaptor. Your personal connection to the material, as well as your ability to define that thematic connection, will drive your choices of what to keep and what to cut. Language, the second building block, is your playwright's medium, the tool for creating the scenes that follow that theme. The language the script gives your actors to speak, as well as the language in a few well-chosen stage directions and the words you use to evoke your stageable image, will build the bridge between the original page and the waiting stage.

In the following examples, I've chosen plays that are particularly strong in each element. Looking at a familiar play through this lens of the balance of elements may help you to get a feel for how different weights play out.

Example of a Theme-Driven Play (Building Block 1)

Topdog/Underdog by Suzan-Lori Parks
Theme: How we are defined by history.

The parents of two black brothers have named them Lincoln and Booth. The play extends the historical metaphor and thematic humor by having the brothers work at a fair where they reenact Booth's assassination of Lincoln.

Physical action is a key performance vocabulary, especially in the brothers' reenactment, performed in full period costume, complete with the famous Lincoln stovepipe hat.

Example of a Language-Activated Play (Building Block 2)

Travesties by Tom Stoppard
Language: Sumptuous linguistic inventiveness, for which the playwright boldly assumes that the audience listens intently and is well-read and intellectually game.

The language itself reveals characters, ideas, time, and place. Its linguistic daring defines this investigation into literature, art, and politics. *Travesties* weaves the improbable meeting of three historical figures who happen to be in Zurich—V. I. Lenin, James Joyce, and Tristan Tzara (leader of the dadaists)—with encounters of female fictional characters from *The Importance of Being Earnest.*

A key content element is the theme of memory, as the play is set in the faulty memory of Henry Carr during World War I.

Example of a Character-Driven Play (Building Block 3)

Mother Courage and Her Children by Bertolt Brecht
Character: A woman during the Hundred Years' War.

This play is a monumental character study. The woman's instincts for survival battle her need to mother her children. Mother Courage is a character of great contradictions: her name is "courage" yet she is a coward; she parasitically lives off the war with her canteen wagon, yet she shares with those she picks up along the way; and she is a mother who fails to protect her daughter.

The dominant formal element is the image of her cart. It travels throughout the play, stocked with the spoils and salable materials of a war culture. As the mother loses her compatriots and children, she must finally drag the cart on her own.

Example of a Relationship-Driven Play (Building Block 3)

True West by Sam Shepard
Relationship: Antagonistic brothers in a symbiotic relationship.

Lee is a slovenly drifter and small-time cat burglar. Austin is a hip, up-and-coming screenwriter. The estranged, contentious brothers end up housesitting together for their mother in the desert outside Los Angeles. They attempt to reconcile their opposing natures—Lee a romantic, Austin a pragmatist—by agreeing to share their particular gifts. Shepard structures the progression of the relationship so that the two have traded lives by the story's end.

The key form element is Shepard's lyrical, rough, western-myth-inducing dialogue.

Example of an Image-Activated Play (Building Block 4)

Equus by Peter Shaffer
Image: Horses.

The title, *Equus,* is the Latin word for "horse." The main character is a disturbed young boy whose mysterious chanting of this word is the primary clue to understanding why he has destroyed the beloved horses he takes care of. The horses are theatricalized as statuesque actors in horse-shaped sculptural headgear and elevating hooflike boots.

The key content element is character. A psychologist's delving into the hidden secrets of the boy's mind, as the boy grapples with those same inner demons in his yearning but tortured relationship with a girl who also works at the stable, makes this a richly layered character study.

Example of a Play Driven by External Events (Building Block 5)

The Cherry Orchard by Anton Chekhov
External storyline event: The forced selling off of the family
        estate.

Years of living beyond their means have finally caught up with members of the Gayev family as they struggle to accept the fact that they can no longer afford to pay their bills from the land's earnings, even though they remain romantically attached to their beloved cherry orchard. Represented by creditors and land developers, the larger forces of a new world order close in on the family's obsolete lifestyle, as the landed gentry of the nineteenth century gives way to the capitalists and middle class of the twentieth.

The key formal element is the nuanced, subtext-laden, realistic speech Chekhov captures for the various classes.

Example of a Play Driven by Prior Circumstances (Building Block 5)

Crimes of the Heart by Beth Henley

Prior Circumstances: What happened between Babe and Willie Jay? And what actually transpired between Meg and Doc on that night of the hurricane?

This ensemble piece traces the three McGrath sisters and the history of their relationships. Salacious and tender details from their past, both with each other and as individuals, emerge one by one to illuminate and shape the current action of the play.

The primary vehicle for action and discovery in this play is the richly evocative language of these small-town southern women, with their affections, eccentricities, and characteristic idioms.

Example of an Action-Activated Play (Building Block 6)

Noises Off by Michael Frayn

Physical Action: The split-second timing of a slapstick farce.

Constructed like a Restoration comedy on steroids, this play involves technically adept, well-rehearsed actors running through doors with precision timing. The play within a play at the center of the story falls apart as an increasingly chaotic backstage life gets more and more tangled.

Prior circumstance revelations about the history of these characters' past relationships bring the story to its convoluted climax.

Two Case Studies

The following lists summarize the key elements of our two primary study plays: *The Cockfighter* and *The Grapes Of Wrath*. The explanations in this list should all be familiar to you now from explorations into these plays that you've encountered in the corresponding chapters of the book. Here I've highlighted the driving content element and its key performance vocabulary. The purpose of such a summary is to let you see a clarifying juxtaposition of what is most important to your play.

Example: The Grapes of Wrath *Elements*

In adapting John Steinbeck's uniquely structured, large-canvas, critical examination of the myth of the American success story, adaptor-director Frank Galati's strategy was to focus on the Joad family. Here is my distillation of its elements.

1. Theme: A family's Darwinian ability to adapt during a drought and depression in the United States.
2. Language: Spare, working class, regional, prosaic. The narration is reportorial and occasionally lyrical.
3. Characters: Ma, her son Tom, Pa, Rose of Sharon, and other members of the Joad family. Major characters from the novel, such as Preacher Casy, also carry dramatic weight and through-line, but Galati edits, combines, or eliminates other minor characters.
   Relationship: The key content element. Familial bonds are under extraordinary stresses. In particular, the story delves into the relationships between Ma and Tom, Ma and Sharon, Tom and Casy, Pa and Ma.
4. Images, the key formal element: The family home, the car they travel in, work camps, the desert, the Dust Bowl, a river, towns along Route 66 from Oklahoma to California, fruit fields, a campsite.
5. Storyline: The Joads survive seemingly insurmountable catastrophes and create a newly bonded and redefined family.
6. Physical actions: Packing, fighting, nurturing, embracing, death of Casy, walking away, dying.

Here are short phrases, distilled from the list, that focus on the most essential components in Galati's script.

1. Theme: Family survival
2. Language: Spare
3. Character: Tom Joad
    Relationship: Ma and Tom
4. **Image: The car**
5. Storyline: Reforming the family
6. Action: Packing and moving

The script of *The Grapes of Wrath* is well balanced in its form elements. The language is regionally specific and evocative of time and place; the physical actions are challenging to act, design, and witness but still connected to the storyline; and the images of the car, camps, and rain give the text a full-throttle theatricality. In such a close call, my selection of image as the most pivotal communicative mode in the script may reflect my own interests and awareness as much as it reflects the priorities of the adaptation.

Example: The Cockfighter Elements

The theatrical image of cockfighting activates the adaptation of *The Cockfighter* and shapes the character work and production style. As in *The Grapes of Wrath*, family relationships are the key content element.

1. Theme: Parents' attempts to control their son, his reaching puberty, and his breaking away.
2. Language: Rural, blunt, southern colloquialism mixed with poetic authorial insights.
3. Characters: Sonny, the boy emerging toward manhood, is the primary voice and protagonist. Jake, his rough father, is the antagonist. Lily, Sonny's overprotective mother, and Homer, who is Lily's brother and Sonny's uncle, complete the principal characters.
    Relationship: The driving content element. In the relationship web of this nuclear family, the primary conflict is the tug-of-war between father and mother to shape a son's destiny.
4. Image, the key formal element: Locations, all playable in the cockpitlike space, include the family's home; the truck that transports

Jake, Sonny, and the birds; a bar; and the cockfighting ring itself. An important prop is the birds' cages.

5. Storyline: A boy nurtures a pet and then is driven to destroy it.
6. Physical actions: Handling, cockfighting, nurturing, preparing food, tending to the cocks, chasing a truck, eating, cradling, enfolding, blinking, pecking.

The short, focused versions:

1. Theme: Rite of passage
2. Language: Poetically blunt
3. Character: The boy
   Relationship: Family in a tug-of-war
4. **Image: The cockfighting pit**
5. Story: Nurture then destroy
6. Action: Birdlike movements

Having the touchstone of such distillations lets you survey aspects of your adaptation to ensure the balance of elements.

Clarifying the Where and When

When you have hopscotched through a novel, cutting and pasting the essential text to get your story and theme realized, you often leave gaps or holes. Even after filling in essential scenes, you may sense something missing between scenes that would make their flowing together or jumping from one to another clear; that would delineate the logic or pointed illogic of your story. These transitional moments might need to be filled with additional text, a narrator, or some theatrical device such as a sign, lighting to suggest the passage of time, or an actor removing a beard to play his character younger. Surprisingly, it's possible that the play needs nothing more and that as playwrights we can trust the audience's connection to the material and their imagination to sustain their involvement.

Television and film train contemporary audiences to see and absorb visual information quickly. Theater forgets itself when it tries to imitate this approach and becomes too literal in the use of multiple, complex sets in trying to let the audience know where they are. We can leave it to film to give us great detail over quickly shifting transitions by showing the Eiffel Tower one minute and a bayou in Louisiana the next. Theater can instead take advantage of the contemporary audience's increased ability to absorb information quickly and through several performance vocabularies simultaneously. Capitalizing on the audience's visual acuity, theater can create conventions in the staging—acting, costume, lighting, sound, or text references—that guide their imaginations to the next time and place.

Most often shifts from one scene to another work best when they are executed as fluidly as possible. Taking stage time to change the set or move large set props disturbs the active engagement of the audience's experience in real time. Sometimes, however, you do want to interrupt the flow. In my production of Franz Kroetz's *Stallers Farm*, a gutwrenching, politically astute play about a mentally challenged girl on a farm, the actors held their positions at the end of scenes and the lights bumped down to half. Depending on the emotional weight of a scene and what I wanted the audience to stop and consider, the lights would stay at half for three to twelve seconds then slowly fade out or occasionally bump to blackout.

When the brilliant novelist Michael Ondaatje adapted his *Collected Works of Billy the Kid* for the stage, he diminished the evocative, poetic leaps he had made in the book's multiple textual styles—searing prose, inner monologue, poems, penny dreadful novel style, newspaper report—by writing explanatory segues for his play version. To me it diminished the stunning, imagistic form of a great work by assuming that a live audience couldn't follow his novelistic leaps. In the version we did in Boston in the 1970s, my colleagues and I stayed true to his structure and language, finding an authentic voice that did work theatrically. Several years later I was able to discuss our different versions with him, and I assured him that his explanatory segues had served only to oversimplify and distract from his richly associative text. An adaptation truer to the source actually adhered to the imagistic form of his original and found a staging strategy that allowed its audience a similar thrill to a reader's experience of the book. He was at that same moment learning how to let his Booker Prize–winning novel, *The English Patient*, go through its metamorphosis to film and to let the new medium dictate its new telling under writer-director Anthony Minghella.

Tracking Time and Place

Scene changes in a play imply a change of time or place, or both. The draft of your play you now have may include no particular effect to indicate shifts between scenes, and it may not need one. Your script may already be clear enough as it is to leave the rest up to your director and designers about how to achieve those shifts. But if you see that your script leaves confusion about where or when the action is happening and if you need to make those contexts clear, you have a delicious array of choices as to how to accomplish the time and place shifts. Also you may want to create continuity in the feel of your scene transitions or let a certain scene have a surprisingly different feel to its beginning or ending than the others.

Some plays that cover a long span of time in a character's life are able to build in key episodes of the story as cinematic- or fiction-style flashbacks. The timeline of Miller's *Death of a Salesman* covers about eighteen hours from very early one morning to late that night, but within that frame it moves back and forth in time between 1949 and 1932. It also moves its place from the Loman home and yard in Brooklyn to a restaurant, an office, and a Boston hotel. This structure allows the playwright to tell the history of the Loman family through a powerful series of crucial prior circumstance revelations. The vignettes allow not only for narrative of those episodes but also for live action by the characters remembering and reenacting them, such as Biff standing at the door of his father's hotel room. Become clear about the time span and range of locations in your play and think about how you want to delineate changes between them.

Utilizing Your Best Materials and Tools as You Define Shifts

Knowing the driving content element of your piece may help you to decide how to structure these shifts. If your play is a deep study of a particular character, what choices does that prompt in the way you handle your transitions? If your lead character is someone who bursts into rooms with big news, then repeating, mirroring, and contrasting that habit to open scenes might become a touchstone of your transitions. If relationship is your pivotal content and there is a dynamic that defines the story's central relationship—such as silence or touching—that dynamic might give you ideas about how to structure your transitions.

Perhaps even more important is your awareness of performance vocabularies. The expressive tools of language, image and design, or actors' actions are the means the production has for making scene shifts clear, and as playwright you will be using language to mark those moments in the script. Is there a change in the language that makes it clear that the play has moved to a new scene? If you are relying on a designer to create effects in the lights or set that indicate scene shifts, have you given enough information in the script for a designer to know where they happen? Are you relying on actors to make the transitions in front of the audience's eyes?

In utilizing the tools of performance vocabularies to effect these transformations of time and place, don't be afraid to let the audience participate by viewing those moments. Critic Nancy Franklin was actually disappointed at the loss of "most of the deliberately self-conscious stage devices" from the staged to the televised version of Margaret Edson's play *Wit*. As she explained it in a *New Yorker* article about *Angels in America:*

> There is a certain kind of magic in the theatre that can't be repli-
> cated in any other form, and it doesn't depend on the audience's
> not seeing how it's done; it's the fact that you often *can* see how it's
> done—whether it's an actor undergoing a transformation in front
> of you or a set design or a lighting effect—that makes you mar-
> vel. Kushner acknowledges this in his stage notes. Such moments,
> he says, "are to be fully realized, as bits of wonderful *theatrical*
> illusion—which means it's O.K. if the wires show, and maybe it's
> good that they do, but the magic should at the same time be thor-
> oughly amazing." (128)

Knowing your own best mode of expression for your piece, exploit it fully, and don't be afraid to use it in unexpected or boldly theatrical ways.

In my adaptation of *The Cockfighter,* I employ the term *shift* to suggest scene changes, movement from one place or time to another. This is the theatrical equivalent to the "cut" from one scene to another in film. Each shift changes the point of view: we are in the bedroom with the parents, then suddenly in Sonny's room as he awakens. Next we shift to the car and the mother running alongside it, then, shift, we are inside her head as she grieves over losing her boy to the father's influence. This one simple term, *shift,* gave plenty of latitude to the collaborators staging the play, and since I was also directing, I went into the rehearsal with some ideas about how to implement those shifts. Some were already scripted, such as the transformation from Lily to Homer through a change of clothing. Others the actors and I discovered together.

The way we handled the shifts in both productions of *The Cockfighter* allowed us to quickly and succinctly set up the next scene or monologue. I also relied on my driving and defining elements of relationship and image to help me effect these shifts. In the Atlanta production, the three actors sat on a small section of bleachers enclosed by wire mesh. They were tiered over each other, switching places to reflect their relationships as the character interactions forged them: the boy excluding his mother and bonding with the father, the mother transforming into Homer then confronting the father on behalf of the boy. As I played out the image idea of the cockfighting ring in the scene shifts, I continued to play with the visual correlation between the many-armed Shiva of their intertwined bodies and a huge bird spreading its wings. A scene shift was also both a shift in the stage picture that continually took its cues from cockfighting imagery and a shift in the relationship dynamics of the three characters trapped in a cockfighting ring, playing out their domestic struggle. This interplay between the content of relationship and the expressive form of visual image shaped my choices from the drafting of the script through the end of the staging.

Aspirations for the Next Stage

Creativity asks a lot of us: stamina, openness, humility, risk taking, imagination, and the skill to fail bravely or succeed charitably. Creating a new work is both fun and demanding. It allows you to escort a beloved piece of literature down the aisle to a theatrical adaptation, to marry them in the living theater of your aspirations for the piece.

The act of creation entangles our hearts in luminous paradoxes, particularly in theater: at the end of our process of finishing the script, it is also ready to be born as a play in production. For theater to exist, the burning loneliness of the adaptor working in solitude must give way to the varying temperatures of collaboration with other artists. And if your goal is to stay true to your vision of the story you want to tell, then you will feel that birth to be successful when you witness a good production of your adaptation, one that enriches and defines your collaborators, audiences, and critics.

Once you've experienced this marriage and birth, your taste of death will be the bittersweet feeling that theater artists experience on closing night. It's a release to the next project: in your case, the next production of your script or the next adaptation that you have already begun writing. If you've stayed true to your source and yourself, the only mourning you'll feel on leaving a closing night is the new morning of other exciting work.

✦ ✦ ✦ ✦

Construction Exercises for Balancing the Blocks

A. Following the two case study models in this chapter, summarize your building block elements and then distill them down to their essence. Highlight your driving content element and its complimentary key formal element.

1. Theme
2. Language
3. Character
   Relationship
4. Image
5. Storyline
6. Action

B. Test sections of the script. As with all choices, what is saved or lost in transferring from the page to the stage will be experienced only by having actors perform it aloud.

- When you had actors or friends read a section or the entire adaptation, where did you feel engaged and where did you feel bored?
- Ask your readers where they felt lost and most engaged. Let them speak without interrupting them, taking notes on points that seem valid. Do their responses surprise you? Do their responses suggest that you emphasize certain elements more than in the previous version?
- Does your chosen driving element still seem most important? Ask your readers what felt significant to them as they listened.

C. Consider what, if any, major structural changes your script might now need.

- If you need to tighten and focus the adaptation, what would you cut?
- If you need to lengthen, deepen, expand, or explore further, what would you add?
- If you need to make the structure of the story clearer and more evocative, what would you rearrange?
- Notice whether your transitions seem to be working effectively. Focus on at least four moments of scene transition from one time and place to another and decide whether they are clear.

- Remember to consider the possibility that your script is already well structured as it is.

D. If you need to do any rewrites based on A, B, and C, do them now. Try out cuts, additions, reordering, and rephrasing—and implement the changes that make sense to you. Be willing to admit when the script is finished.

E. Format your script on the page, if you haven't already, to a standard layout that fellow artists can recognize and work with easily. There are word-processing programs for playwriting that will provide the template of a correctly formatted script for you.

F. Consider asking a theater artist to read your script and give you feedback. If you can find a dramaturg whose opinion you trust, this can be a good jump into working with collaborators. Evaluate any feedback you receive to decide what is true to your vision of the play and what is worth implementing.

G. Now it's time to lift your adaptation onto a stage.

- Do some research to find out which theaters in your area develop new plays. A great place to start is to go see shows and learn about the programs of the theaters while you're there. Check them out on the web as well and talk to anyone you know who can tell you more about theaters that look like a promising match for you.

- Personal contact with appropriate theaters or playlabs is often crucial to getting your words heard. Supporting the work of a local company puts you in its favor. Most theaters are vastly understaffed and overstressed; volunteering to help out will give staff members more incentive to read and respond to your work, and you'll increase the likelihood that you'll find someone to give your play a reading or a workshop.

- If you send a script to an artistic director, literary manager, or new play director blind, be sure to include a note as to why you think your work is a good fit with the mission of the company. If you can't see a production there, then use the company's website or promotional materials to research its interests. Show familiarity with the members' work, just as you hope that they will become familiar with yours by reading your play. By citing knowledge of their productions, you show a connection to their mission and thereby make them more open to collaborating with you.

8

Two Case Studies

Enough and *Me and My Shadow*

To give you a glimpse of the myriad ways that the details can play out in the process of adapting literature, this chapter takes you through case studies of two of my own adaptations. My initial engagement with the first, *Enough,* evolved from both happy accidents and my proactively finding collaborators. Beginning in the late 1970s and continuing into the early 1990s, the script was produced in three distinct versions as I returned to the material to reengage more than once with the personal connection that had first attracted me.

The opportunity to adapt the second case-study piece analyzed here, *Me and My Shadow,* emerged from working with the medley of collaborating artists at Theater Works, the company I cofounded in the 1980s, which became a lab for formulating and creating adaptations. In my capacity as co–artistic director, I functioned as an "auteur" adaptor-director for John Barth's story "Petition" to create this piece.

Through projects we generated at Theater Works, my challenging and creative colleagues and students helped me see the essential elements of play building. Discovering the process and letting each project dictate the approach, I began to detect patterns in the construction— approaches that eventually crystallized into what I now refer to as the building blocks. My Boston colleagues, that construction crew of artists and craftspeople, generated the pieces on which the following two case studies are based.

As you read about my quest to create a workable adaptation by following clues in the text and unleashing my imagination, I hope you'll gain insight into the process and see how it plays out, sometimes in idiosyncratic ways.

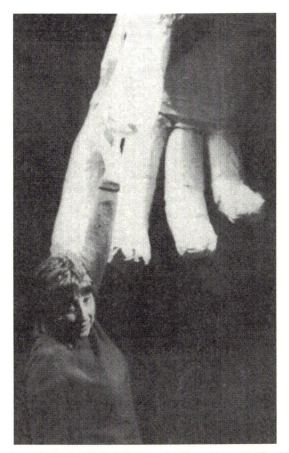

Fig. 9. *Enough*. Newlyweds holding hands. (Sona Grant, Reality Theater, 1978.)

The First *Enough*—Boston, 1979–80: Reality Theater

I am in my late twenties. Two actors from New York ask me to choose a Samuel Beckett play and direct them in it for a festival in Ireland. I'm game. I avidly read the plays, but, perhaps too young for them, I am unable to find one that I connect with, that speaks to my sensibility. I press on by reading the novels, with the weight of Beckett's bleak beauty still leaving me on the outside looking into a world beyond my experience and understanding.

But then, in his short story collection *First Love and Other Shorts,* I finally encounter "Enough," the story of a woman absorbed into the wants and desires of her husband. The woman even seems to walk out of his life when he asks her to leave him. It's an archetypal story that reminds me of the women who were reabsorbed into their husbands' male-oriented world after World War II, who experienced a sea change that seeped into their consciousness, and who one day went out on their own. My mother's story. I hear my mother's voice in the words.

Admitting my failure to find an existing script for the New York actors, I stop planning the trip to Ireland and go in search of the play within this story.

I read "Enough" to my mother. She says that she *is* this woman, that the play speaks to the silence that she and other women carried as their husbands returned from World War II full of rage, wounds, and shock, full of a terrible, dangerous daily life of war, hard to reconcile with middle-class domesticity.

I work on the adaptation.

From my rereadings of the text and brainstorming with an actor friend, the evocative stageable image emerges: one person being absorbed by another, a woman by a man. In her words, "All I know comes from him." For the production, I want an environment that employs American folk art to evoke the world of the husband, since the feeling of "Enough" seems close to some folk art pieces I've seen: the placid, blunt surfaces, the eerie silence, the shifting scale. To create the absorption image, I do research and consult with visual artists and magicians.

I look for other collaborators. I have involved myself in the local theater community by acting at a few theaters, teaching part-time at area colleges, and directing and acting with the collective Reality Theater, which runs its own theater school. At the University of Massachusetts Boston, where I teach directing and playwriting, I have three older, exceptional students who collaborated on a show I directed there. After a class at U. Mass I run into one of them, Donald Meuse, and we start brainstorming about the Beckett text, folk art, and how to realize the husband. An extremely gifted visual artist, Donald then does research into folk art and thinks about the husband question, and he comes back a week later with sketches, which eventually lead to the final design.

Casting, Producing, and Permission

The success of the adaptation in performance will rest on finding an actress capable of handling the language while evoking the relationship with her dominating husband, whom she, at least in her mind, is leaving.

I find the woman to play the part when I meet with Sona Grant, a spirited, smart, older actress I've seen onstage at another local theater where I have also acted. She has the Beckettian qualities of seeming at once haunted and full of humor, of a capacity for silence, and of a tongue that speaks spare, brutal beauty. Reading the part for me, she shows the vulnerability and intelligence that the role demands. As I ask her questions about the role and we discuss the piece, her insights and convictions about the material convince me to cast her.

Who will produce it? Me. I pitch the idea to the Reality Theater Company, a group of experimental theater aficionados who work collectively, encourage new work, and seek out projects from their members, of which I'm one. We have access to a performance space, across from Fenway Park at the Massachusetts College of Art, that is workable for the scale of visual-art-dominated design that Don and I have devised. The limited budget for the show forces us to be inventive. The three talented U. Mass students dive into a brave new world of set, prop, costume, and sound design that incorporates the image of a woman who has been absorbed into a man and then breaks away. With Reality Theater's help, including a five-hundred-dollar budget that we supplement with our own money, we develop the project over eight weeks while also working at our part-time jobs, completing school assignments, and tending to our relationships.

Meanwhile, I pursue the rights to adapt the material, promising to play it without cuts or reorganization, both by writing to Beckett's agent and by sending him a request through actors at the Open Theater of New York who would be performing one of his plays in Paris, which he is to attend. At this time in his career, Beckett is notorious for not allowing his nondramatic material to be theatricalized without his direct participation. My requests via Paris and to the agent are never answered.

Playing word-for-word with the text and incorporating the discoveries made with my collaborators, I finish the adaptation and direct a production set in a giant folk art world with enormous silent cats and a disconnected man's body for the woman to be lost in. We open the production to critical acclaim, but a cease-and-desist order from Beckett's lawyers closes it in the third week, with the news that they will not grant permission for the production.

The Six Building Blocks for the First *Enough*

We can use the template of the six building blocks to track guiding discoveries I made about the form and content of *Enough* during the process of adapting it.

1. Material and theme: I'm compelled to tell my mother's story of a woman absorbed by a man and the discovery of a self.
2. Language:
     "I did all he desired. I desired it too. For him. Whenever he desired something so did I. He only had to say what thing." "We were on the whole calm. More and more. All was. This notion of calm comes from him. Without him I would not have had it. Now I'll wipe out everything but the flowers. No more rain. No more mounds. Nothing but the two of us dragging through the flowers. Enough my old breasts feel his old hand."
3. Characters: Principal character is the woman, who is old but in memory is at times a young girl. The secondary character is the husband, prone in bed and at times glimpsed in her memory. He is represented by oversized body parts, not an actor.
     Relationship: A submissive wife and a controlling husband; the woman's attempt to control her own body and needs in a marriage; forgetting, having enough.
4. Images: Inside the woman's mind, at bedside, in the mountains, star constellations, a horizon, a door, a mound, large male body parts, folk art cats and dogs.
5. Storyline: A woman sheds her husband's imprint and becomes herself.
6. Physical actions: Stepping on flowers; a larger male hand holding a small white-gloved hand; the woman's hands walking with very large men's shoes on them, her ex-husband's "feet" creating syncopation with her walking, slowing down, and bending; the woman stepping away.

This first production of the adaptation focused on the content element of the character of the woman, set in a world where her husband would absorb her. The design images were pivotal to the production— the driving performance vocabulary. I also wanted to make the climbing an important action, as well as the growing and destroying of the flowers. My research led me to incorporate American folk art dolls and magicians' tricks in which people disappear. A scenographer designed an environment where the woman could be absorbed or made tiny: a six-foot man's hand reached down from the ceiling; an eight-foot, soft-sculptured man's foot could become either a bed, a companion to walk with, or a mound going up as it stepped. A pair of three-foot lips had a small curtain for teeth that opened to reveal a puppet body with the head of a man's penis dancing to the English music hall renditions of Gracie Fields. These design elements captured the evocative stageable image of a woman's absorption into a man.

In its review of the production, the *Boston Globe* called it "a highly visual/aural theater piece" that "found the often overlooked (or simply misunderstood) clue to Beckett. Which is humor," albeit through what the reviewer considered to be "outrageous dramatic license" in giving the woman "a stream of fantasies slightly indicated on the page; fantasies realized through jaunty old recorded songs by Gracie Fields." The reviewer cited as the "most inspired moment" the one in which the actress, "wearing her husband's battered black shoes on her hands, marches them up and down while standing in place and staring out into the endless, beckoning void."

In my stubborn determination to stay true to the evocative stageable image of absorption, I was lucky to have collaborators who were intuitive and gutsy enough to make it work. The images we discovered in developing this production continue to live with me to this day, and it was a pivotal moment in deepening my understanding of the adaptation process and how to trust the theatricality of literary texts.

Second *Enough*—Boston, 1984: Theater Works

Revisiting a cherished work of literature is one of the great pleasures of sustaining a career as an artist. The work can be a litmus test of your values, cares, and maturity. It can also test your courage to go further or to humbly admit what the text can accomplish by simply being acted well. In the next two decades, I devised radically different notions for productions of the *Enough* script that were given permission by Beckett's agents.

As I prepare for the second production some years later, the clues in the text lead me to a performance in which the opening line, "All that goes before forget"—the event of memory—takes focus. We bring the husband and the various ages of the woman onstage by not only casting the man as a live actor but also by casting two actresses—one older and one younger—to share the role of the woman and play her at both present and remembered ages.

Peeling the layers of memory becomes the evocative stageable image. Paul Shakespear, a gifted visual artist, realizes the image by covering a large wall with turn-of-the-century wallpaper that is torn away, peeling, or faded with age to reveal the complex interior of the woman's memory

Fig. 10. *Enough.* The husband younger and wife both older and younger remember each other. (Jim Kaufman, Joan Gale, and Kirsten Giroux, Theater Works, 1982.)

and experience. Either the young woman or the older version speaks the narrative in front of the wall while her other self is behind it doing domestic chores or playing actions of leaving, crushing, disappearing, or submitting. She is sometimes alone, sometimes with the husband.

While the first production focused more on the character of the woman, this version focuses on the relationship of the woman to her husband. Like the first, this production strives for a theatricality that turns the theater into the woman's memory box. Images that are described in the source material are staged in the performance, such as the character posture of the man sagging at the knees, the woman's monumental first step, or the wiping out of the flowers.

The Six Building Blocks for the Second *Enough*

1. Theme: The reality of memory
2. Language: "I cannot have been more than six when he took me by the hand."

   "[H]e held his legs apart and sagged at the knees. His feet grew more and more flat and splay."

3. Characters: Younger and older versions of the woman; her husband. Relationship: That of an unformed wife and her demanding, needy husband.
4. Images: A wall of peeling nineteenth-century wallpaper that peels away or covers scenes as they occur. Varying voices to evoke the sounds of youth or aging.
5. Storyline: A woman sees herself change throughout her life.
6. Physical actions: Moving in old or young ways, taking steps, holding hands, his wrapping himself around her.

The look and feel of the second production were vastly different from those of the first. Some regulars at our theater thought it was a new text. The style became more severe yet more hellzapoppin, with the quick snapshots that the multiple actors and peel-away set generated. This version put aside the edgy humor and existential ache of the first and gained depth in the married relationship and a more vibrantly manifest history for the home life of the couple. The peeling layers of memory became the evocative stageable image, which then drove the multiple casting and notion of aging in the production.

A lovely feature of this interpretation was the cubistlike sensation of seeing and hearing multiple perspectives at the same moment: the woman seen as both old and young, the memories both ancient and present. The split casting of the woman and the casting of a single actor as the husband did, however, diminish the distinctive single point of view of an older woman and too often made entertaining stage pictures at the expense of offering one woman's journey. It worked best when the two women merged their voices and side lighting created a half face of each. Yet, while the multiple casting gave us a more vivid picture of the marriage, it muted the achingly embedded point of view of an older woman working out what happened on her own. The fracturing of the younger and older woman and the disappearing husband undercut the power of the audience to project and imagine the events that lead the woman to walk away.

Third *Enough*—Atlanta and the Netherlands, 1991: Theater Emory

A decade later I produce Brenda Bynum's Theater Emory production of *A Stain on a Silence*, a staging of a collection of short Beckett plays. The distillation that Beckett requires lives in this actress. Older, and perhaps

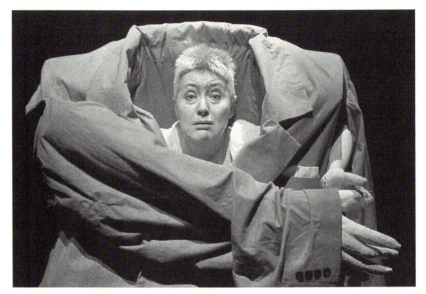

Fig. 11. *Enough.* The woman buried in her husband's greatcoat. (Brenda Bynum, Theater Emory, 1992.)

less in need of spicing Beckett's text with my theatricality, I return to the absorption metaphor. With a single actor and new collaborators, I set out to create a production that lets the text and action be more present but stripped down: a footstep or the tilt of a head will suffice for a dramatic event.

Over the next year I work with a talented designer to imagine a staging with an enormous male puppet encompassing the woman and a door leading to the road where she will take her first independent step. The zeroing-in process guides me to the image of a man's greatcoat, which swallows the woman yet eventually opens up to create a road. The actor is placed inside an enormous, freestanding man's greatcoat—her arms manipulating the longer male puppet arms, her head appearing tiny within the collar of the coat. Eventually the coat opens and unfurls into a pathway, with each step a measured action away. When she takes that step, the lighting leaves the massive silhouette of her husband behind her.

The Six Building Blocks for the Third *Enough*

1. Theme: A crucial turning point.
2. Language: "One day he told me to leave him. It's the verb he used. He must have been on his last legs. I don't know if by that he meant me to leave him for good or only step aside a moment. I never asked myself the question. I never asked any question but his. Whatever it was he meant I made off without looking back." (203)
3. Characters: The woman. In this production, like the first, I returned to representing the man with design elements, some of which the woman herself could manipulate, essentially as a puppeteer.
   Relationship: A marriage that is encasing, entombing, and immobilizing the woman.
4. Images: A great overcoat that becomes a road.
5. Storyline: Seeing yourself taking an important step away.
6. Physical actions: Unbuttoning, pushing forward, an arm to the woman's breast.

This third production premiered at the International Beckett Festival in The Hague, Holland, and the evocative severity of this staging met with acclaim from the scholars and critics who attended. The vocal texture and actions embedded in the language became a delicious, enriching experience offered by Brenda Bynum, an actress of great aural skill. The husband that consumed her was expertly realized in an evocative set by Leslie Taylor: a massive greatcoat, allowing the collaborators to focus on how this relationship both gave her identity and engendered an eventual need to break away from its shackles (see Figure 11).

In his review of the production, Dan Hulbert of the *Atlanta Journal-Constitution* noted the "giant coat, charged with life as it bears the rumples and bulges of the man who wore it" and described the way "Ms. Bynum's head pops out of the collar, like a chipmunk from the hollow of a massive oak." He called the coat "exactly the vivid image needed in this Vincent Murphy adaptation to crystallize a text which (like much of Beckett's late work) is as elusive and sketchy as it is poignant and profound." Testifying to the success of our use of the enormous coat as our evocative stageable image, he saw it as a manifest metaphor of "an unnamed woman who literally was absorbed into her dominating husband, and now dwells in memories of him, much as she inhabits the coat."

As these three productions attest, even a single adaptor, over time, will read a piece of literature and imagine its theatrical possibilities differently. As much as we respond to the theme, character, or storyline, we also respond to the place in which we live and the collaborators we have chosen to create the world of the play. The first *Enough* was driven by my desire to open up a Beckett text to a visual art environment; the second by a company of actors at Theater Works and an insightful painter who had the powerful idea of a peeling Victorian wallpaper through which to see the actors; and the third dominated by an intimate space, the need to transport the production to Europe, and an actor who could move in the stillness and voice the silence.

"Petition"/Me and My Shadow—Boston, 1982

In the author's note that prefaces his collection of short stories *Lost in the Funhouse,* John Barth describes this story as a piece impossible to translate from one medium to another. He writes that some of his other stories might work as radio plays, animations, reader's theater, or stage plays; indeed, he challenges his readers to imagine the stories not only read silently but also spoken aloud. But "Petition," he insists, is one of the pieces that can work only as literature, that would "lose part of their point in any except printed form."

Attempting this ostensibly impossible adaptation is a great creative challenge. Directing *Enough* has given me the courage to believe that language-rich texts can be successful onstage if I can find evocative theatricality and inventive actors.

My cofounder in Theater Works is actor Tim McDonough. We have acted together at the Cambridge Ensemble, and I've directed him at Reality Theater. I realize that he is uniquely able to play the central role of the back brother for our company. As we explore this Barth story, he clarifies how the text's narrative point of view can fluidly shift from first person to third to omniscient while remaining in balance with the existential sideshow. In this production, as in many that will come in the future, he is a fearless collaborator. His only reluctance comes when I ask him to shave his head. Two other talented actors who are principal members of the company, Kirsten Giroux and Kathleen Patrick, will jointly play the role of Thalia, the contortionist.

What I discover as we investigate this story is that ostensibly impossible texts are possible when you break the conventional mold that limits

Fig. 12. *Me and My Shadow.* Passing confidences. (Bill McCann, Tim McDonough, and Kathy Patrick. Theater Works, 1982.)

the way theater artists collaborate with each other and with other disciplines. One needs to stay imaginatively open to the particularities and peculiarities of the work at hand. The text must lead. And an adaptor must find a strong staging metaphor that challenges the imagination and surpasses the ready-made geography of naturalistic blocking, decorative set design, and acting mired in reductive pop psychology. The breakthrough in this research is in finding a representational method of portraying the multilayered, more complex psychological reality of one of the twins by evoking his world of dualities, a reality made manifest by creating an evocative stageable image that captures this theme by manifesting its metaphor in physical space.

Speaking the Speech, and to Whom

The seemingly insurmountable task of adapting this piece rests on the one-man narrative, which presents the story of "Petition" in the form of a letter. Eng, the back brother of attached Siamese twins, is writing a plea to the visiting king of Siam to help him be surgically separated from his brother. The language of the petition is dazzling: beautiful, long, complex sentences in a uniquely erudite yet innocent voice. In an odd-couple juxtaposition of two disparate characters, the front twin brother, Chang, is gross and oversexed, as compared to the back brother, Eng, who is pristine and introspective. The two of them are touring on the sideshow circuit with a shared love interest, a contortionist named Thalia.

Barth writes complex, deliciously baroque sentences as pleasurable to read as to hear. The form of the petition is an engaging dramatic plea with a ready beginning, middle, and end. This structure allows me to leave the original narrative intact, word for word, in the adaptation. Since the back brother is pleading his case to a king sitting in judgment, I make the theatrical choice for Eng to play it presentationally to the audience, whose members then become the king of Siam. Such a choice about who a character is speaking to can often lead to revealing possibilities in the staging and acting. Making the audience the king prompts Tim, as the back brother, to find opportunities to appeal directly to them in pleading his case.

Excerpts from "Petition" by John Barth

"Vain dreams; we are nothing alike. I am slight, my brother is gross. He's incoherent but vocal; I'm articulate and mute. He's ignorant but full of guile; I think I may call myself reasonably educated, and if ingenuous, no more so I hope than the run of scholars. My brother is gregarious: he deals with the public; earns and spends our income; tends (but slovenly) the house and grounds; makes, entertains, and loses friends; indulges in hobbies; pursues ambitions and women" (62).

And, "In earliest babyhood I didn't realize I was two; it was the intractability of that creature always before me—going left when I would go right, bawling for food when I would sleep, laughing when I wept—that opened my eyes to the possibility he was other than myself; the teasing of playmates, who mocked our contretemps, verified that suspicion, and I began my painful schooling in detachment" (62).

The leap from literature to theater involves an act of imagination based on the clues in the text. I doubt that any two adaptors would read even the same stated clues and reach a similar notion of the theatrical world of a story or focus on the same evocative stageable image.

Clues to Finding the Evocative Stageable Image

Committed to a faithful rendering of the text, I follow the clues in the theme, language, character, storyline, and action to unearth several leads toward a possible central image.

1. Eng alone on stage with a single spotlight pleading with the king of Siam.
2. Eng with a "puppet brother" attached to his chest, which he manipulates while pleading.
3. Actors playing Chang, Eng, the contortionist, and the Master of Ceremonies.
4. A circus sideshow.

I can imagine how any one of these possibilities will allow the text to be played uncut, principally in the voice of Eng, as the whole of the action occurs inside his mind. Considering these options leads me to naming an evocative stageable image that will allow me to include most of these images as design elements in the production: a sideshow world of duality. The idea of a circus sideshow of the 1920s gives me the basis for research into a style for the set, costumes, makeup, lighting, and performable routines. Incorporating the idea of duality in naming the central staging metaphor keeps me focused on my chosen theme, which has stayed with me since my first reading of the story. Now, in adapting "Petition" to the stage, I hope to find a theatrical vocabulary that evokes the dualities that struck me initially.

I set out to capture the story's apocalyptic vaudeville tone by creating a production vocabulary of an imaginary, existential circus sideshow based on this evocative stageable image. My research takes me into German cabaret, the psychology of multiple personalities, strip-club exotica, and a trip to Vermont to the Bread and Puppet Theater to see how I might integrate actor physicalizing with the use of puppets.

Staying Open to Finding Collaborators

Directing another show in Vancouver while I am creating the adaptation of "Petition," I meet William Zimmerman, an engineer trained at MIT and a very imaginative scenic designer. Informally we brainstorm on "Petition," and he invites me to pursue a collaboration on Great Island in Nova Scotia, where he lives and owns an artists' retreat. His research skills and collaborative flexibility convince me to hire him to come to Boston to create the piece. Bill adroitly manages to balance several production needs to create a theatrical environment for this narrative. Since the adaptation focuses on multiple characters that coexist in a sideshow circus, the Siamese twin brothers and the woman contortionist need to appear and disappear quickly on the sideshow stage. His ingenious and conveniently inexpensive solution is based on a circular, tilted platform, eighteen feet in diameter. A curtain of clear beads cuts across the top third of the platform and allows me to stage the counterpointing vaudevillelike acts of duality behind the bead scrim. A seat is hinged to a trap door, so it can flip over and disappear. The evocative staging image of an existential sideshow allows the actors and costume and lighting designers expansive options for realizing the staging.

In my research into possible elements of the sound design, I listen to the music of the 1920s, including circus music, jazz, German cabaret, show tunes, and pop. I hear a rendition of a 1927 song with lyrics by Billy Rose: "Me and My Shadow," by Al Jolson and Dave Dreyer. Its melody and playful tone and the tantalizing theatricality of its title significantly shape my ideas about the production, as well as its final form. The song becomes a touchstone of the adaptation, as we employ various recordings of it to underscore the vaudeville routines and segue between scenes. I rechristen the adaptation version with the title *Me and My Shadow.*

The Six Building Blocks for "Petition"/*Me and My Shadow*

1. Theme: Duality—the struggle of siblings, the powerlessness to control our own lives, and the intrinsic conflicts within our dual natures— sexual yet puritanical, voracious yet generous, brutal yet kind.
2. Language: "I am by nature withdrawn, even solitary: an observer of life, a mediator, a taker of notes, a dreamer if you will—yet not a brooder; it's he who moods and broods, today hilarious, tomorrow despondent; I myself am stoical, detached as it were—of necessity, or I'd have long since perished of despair." (64)
3. Characters: Eng, the sensitive back brother, is the principal character and protagonist, whose narrative voice, point of view, and plight carry the story. The front brother, Chang, is the antagonist. The other characters are the contortionist, who is the focus of the love story, and the Master of Ceremonies for the touring sideshows.

Relationships: The most important is between the brothers, biologically joined but opposite in temperament. Next are their two different relationships with their love interest, the contortionist.

4. Images: Circus sideshow touring the United States, twins, mirrors, writing on walls.
5. Storyline: A man confronts his dual nature: the back brother's years of dealing with his grotesque other half.
6. Physical actions: Disappearing, the front brother's grabbing and shaking his brother or putting silly hats on him, the back brother's falling to his knees.

One of the pleasures in meeting National Book Award–winning writer John Barth on a visit to see his short story adapted into a play was his acknowledgment that he had tried unsuccessfully to write a play and thought "Petition" could never become one. But this "impossible" adaptation challenge turned out to be not only workable but a career highlight for me. Several elements were, in retrospect, crucial to its success: casting an actor who could adroitly voice the complex text; cultivating designers who could envision the thematic dualities in realizable set, costume, sound, and lighting choices; and casting mercurial supporting actors who could shift personas, performing styles, and points of view at a finger snap.

The opposite lessons I learned from these two productions—that less was more in *Enough* and that *Me and My Shadow* only worked with more—provided fertile soil for the building blocks of adaptation. To construct a workable play from the materials of literature, you build both by following your intuition and by specifying what tool is primary in creating a foundation other collaborators can also build on. Like an architect with a blueprint or a sculptor with a mound of clay, your charge is to decide where to begin.

9

Partnership and Performance

Theater demands collaboration. It is a meeting of author's text, designer's vision, and director's staging in the real space where actor and audience encounter one another. Theater is not an interior esthetic experience like reading a novel or even a play. It is a communal joining at the place where the imagination of the writer is given flesh on the stage. To accomplish this manifestation of the story in three dimensions, you as the writer must work with a theater that can develop or produce your work.

Building Collaborative Relationships

Companies all over the country function as incubators for literary adaptations. In theaters' new play labs, reading series, or in-house workshops, people can find feedback for their literary adaptations in progress. Depending on a theater's mission and resources, you must expect to show initiative and stamina in getting from the page to the stage. A play lab devoted to developing scripts, such as Austin Scriptworks, has limited resources but will be singularly focused on your work. A large regional theater will have more resources, although the attention your adaptation gets will depend on how savvy its new play person is in developing material in an organization with multiple missions.

The Cockfighter, for example, had its first workshop at the Horizon Theater, a midsized Atlanta company (with an annual operating budget of over $500,000). After I had adapted the work and it was ready for this first professional reading, I applied for a small grant from the Fulton County Arts Council, which gave me four hundred dollars to pay these actors for a two-day workshop. For the next stage in the script's creation,

I negotiated a bare-bones production at PushPush Theater, a small company (with an annual operating budget of under $150,000) that focuses on unique collaborations. With limited staff and resources, I functioned as a coproducer, adaptor, director, stage manager, set designer, and prop crew. The play was then selected by the Actors Theatre of Louisville's Humana Festival of New American Plays for a full professional production and lavish attention.

The path of a talented young playwright born in Atlanta, Lauren Gunderson, illustrates how one can build collaborative relationships in theater. She cultivated connections to the local theater community and thus created inroads to getting her plays produced. While still in high school, she volunteered at local theaters, took workshops, and eventually was cast as an actor to play young roles. When she wrote a travel play about the South, she was able to persuade members of the theater community to read it and give her feedback. She submitted it to playwriting contests and won a playwriting award, given to a Georgia native, from the Essential Theatre of Atlanta. The prize included funding for a professional production of the play, which gave her new insights into her script. Her rewrite was then accepted at the prestigious Young Playwrights festival in New York and staged as a fully realized Equity production. She continued to connect to theater people when she became a theater and creative writing major at Emory, and she was able to mine the professional expertise available to her, tap into the resources of a university drama department—often a good resource for a new playwright—and get her writing workshopped and produced while she was an undergraduate. Her success there led to other productions, publication, and major playwriting commissions.

Regional theaters are the locus of the development for most plays that go on to Broadway or the international circuit. For example, August Wilson developed most of his ten-play cycle at the Playwrights' Center in Minneapolis and the Yale Repertory Theatre.

The best collaborations aspire to share the most inspired ideas and choices rather than reducing the text to a canvas stretched thin between the individual players' limited proprietary needs and notions. The collaborative process is often both thrilling and enervating, at times within seconds, and the skill of guiding talented colleagues can require a teacher's patience, a CEO's authority, a reporter's acumen in asking questions, and a diplomat's skill in sorting through all the input to arrive at an inspired piece. The process is almost always worth the investment. As a playwright workshopping an unfinished play, an adaptor needs to stay true to the impulses that encouraged the initial creative step. Keeping a clear storyline, theme, and evocative stageable image will keep you grounded.

My own experience of developing plays collaboratively has evolved through joining companies where creating together is highly valued. Many of the adaptations that I have developed were created in close collaboration with other theater artists whose contributions have shaped the final script and performance in fundamental, transformative ways.

As I described in the introduction, it was seeing a performance produced by Joseph Chaikin's Open Theater Company that transformed my notions of what theater could be. True to its name, it opened my mind to unexpected possibilities. In college I had created a theater company where I could experiment with innovative approaches to making plays, happily failing or succeeding with wonder. I was fortunate to get to actually work and study with the members of the Open Theater not long afterward, and they also blew open my ideas about how theater can be created as I learned their intensely collaborative workshop process, which focused on working with playwrights and on empowering the actors in the adaptation process. There I witnessed how the synergy of collaboration can create a critical mass of clarity that is not possible in solo work. When I later cofounded a theater company in Boston with Tim McDonough, we made collaborative creation through the workshop process a cornerstone of our mission.

The Workshop Process

Adaptations are uniquely well suited to the collaborative developmental process of the workshop, because the artists coming to the project can share a clearly defined starting point: the original text. A workshop seeks a collective brainstorm to evoke the world of the play—a storm of questions, answers, and intuitions captured to be made manifest. Does the piece have one style or a mix? Should the words be spoken, sung, or played as an action? What is the balance of the elements in the text among music, acting, design, staging, or expectations of the audience's imagination? Whereas rehearsal is often about getting the work right, a workshop is about making it clearer. In a workshop you must be brave to offer what you think is helpful and set your ego aside when another collaborator has a better idea or strategy.

In a workshop, at its best, multiple collaborators aspire to discover and share the most inspired ideas and choices to create the world of a play, regardless of who contributes them. In a workshop, there is no production date set, so a rehearsal process has not yet begun. The collaborators come to the process with defined roles—playwright, director, designer, dramaturg, composer, actor—and each artist is likely to bring a particular expertise to the workshop. But during this unique exploration of the play, the roles remain fluid as all reach out from a position of learning and discovery. In creating something new and uncovering what is unique to the world they are creating, the collaborators allow the boundaries between their disciplines to open and overlap. An actor might hit on a powerful possibility for an evocative stageable image, a director might find a melody line that becomes the basis for a song, a designer could discover a choreographic movement that captures a scene, or a dramaturg might read a monologue with a cadence that gives it new dimensions.

If the script continues toward a full production, a rehearsal process will come later. Rehearsals, unlike workshops, are about defining your role in relationship to others. The playwright writes, the director stages, the actor plays action, the dramaturg contextualizes—each contributor has a bottom-line responsibility for a particular aspect of the production and focuses on that facet of the work in what is often an intense, time-pressured rehearsal period. But in a successful workshop the roles retain a mutability that allows artists to talk across their usual boundaries. Ideally, anyone could take any role at any moment. As many of us are trained to be proprietary about our assigned roles, the challenge of mutual creation can be unnerving. We also face the pressure of our dogged individuality and the solo ownership of work, during a process that demands collectivity.

Having opened themselves to the others' contributions, each of the collaborators still assumes primary responsibility for assimilating the information relevant to their role as actor, designer, and so on and for flagging their coworkers if the input becomes too much for or disruptive of their process. Then they can put one hand up, like Diana Ross of the Supremes, and say, "Stop in the name of love."

The director functions as a conductor: clarifying the tone, emphasis, and balance among the players, all in careful tandem with the playwright if the workshop is developing new material with and for a playwright constructing a script. A talented director can blend several opinionated artists' perspectives into a work that makes the parts into a greater whole.

Some of you may have already been using this book as a guide for a group, rather than an individual, to create an adaptation—which I highly recommend. In a group you can divvy up the exercises at the end of each chapter and then combine the results, perhaps speeding up the process considerably. Or you can work in parallel on the same text, each doing the same homework and then comparing your notes to choose which ideas you all like best. You can also bring the questions themselves into live workshop time and see where they lead you.

The Auteur Model of the Adaptor-Director

Auteur first appeared in English as a term to describe a film director whose style and control of most aspects of a film make him or her a film's "author," its primary originator. In a different tradition from theater's relationship to playwrights, writers in film often are relegated to a secondary status, as the technical needs of telling a story on film require a sensibility more visual than literary. Francois Truffaut, Wong Kar-Wai, Lars von Trier, Nora Ephron, Quentin Tarantino, and Sally Potter are some of our foremost auteurs: they write, direct, and leave an indelible signature style in their work.

An auteur assumes the responsibilities of multiple collaborators. Dispensing with the necessity of meeting and finding common ground with other significant contributors—such as a director or lead actor or perhaps a designer or editor—can be liberating. Auteurs need not articulate ground rules or a common vocabulary while developing the work. They are free to follow their intuitions: if one aspect seems out of balance, such as the character traits of the antagonist, they can decide to put more emphasis on the story of the protagonist.

Because the camera can, and indeed must, guide the eye of the audience much more precisely than an open stage can, an auteur in film can effectively exercise a great deal of control over the finished production, even to the point of editing out scenes if they don't fit his or her vision of the final cut. And the upside of the auteur method, with its combination writer-director, is the single unifying vision that one artist can bring to a project to focus it. Having written the piece, the director is then intimately familiar with the material—not only its words but also its unwritten nuances. Ideas that did not appear in the script can be played out in detail through design choices, direction to the actors, or cinematography decisions that the auteur has kept in mind throughout the process of creation. Assuming responsibilities that might have been delegated to other collaborators, all in order to manifest a comprehensive vision that elevates the parts into a greater whole, is what distinguishes the great auteur.

In theater, the prevailing wisdom is that playwrights should not direct their own plays. Writers work alone, from specific experiences they long to elevate to an art that speaks to many. The intricate task of balancing the needs of the text with the demands of casting, staging, and guiding a full production is not for the fainthearted. And the playwright often holds a deep attachment to the sanctity of the words, as well as, on occasion, to visceral notions of how the characters look, sound, and act. The great majority of writers find the director's role of coaching performances and rallying the many collaborators to find a unifying performance scheme too daunting, and they are pleased to be able to turn their scripts over to someone who has developed this distinct set of skills.

Challenges That Multitasking Adaptors Face

Adaptors who also direct face unique challenges. Authoring the adaptation is challenging enough. And if you are involved in a collaborative workshop process to develop a script you have adapted, you also may be rewriting some sections of it, offering new scenes, and incorporating what you are discovering from a fruitful collaboration. Such shaping of the text during an active collaboration among actors, designers, producers, and a director already takes formidable stamina and imagination. And you may know the material so well that you fail to see what doesn't work on its feet. Or, to name a few of the potential pitfalls of trying your hand at directing, you may not be well versed in the most effective ways to cast actors, work with designers, or build a schedule that accommodates the myriad collaborators in a constructive rhythm.

Occasionally, instead of or in addition to assuming the role of director, the adaptor will take on another significant role in the collaboration, whether as actor, designer, or producer. In theater perhaps the ultimate exercise in auteurship is the one-woman or one-man show, which often evolves from an actor's desire to create a play based on a book or story, and for which an actor may be willing to write the adaptation, create the physical design, act, and wear any other hats needed to bring the piece to an audience.

Some Auteurs and the Theater Companies That Have Kept Them

As an inherently collaborative art form, theater prescribes the limits of auteurship, and it seems that almost all significant adaptations directed by the adaptor succeed due to a collaborative relationship with a theater company. Although the adaptor-director can shape most of the vision of a piece, having a company with members who regularly collaborate gives the adaptor-director a group with a working vocabulary in design, acting, dramaturgy, and community understanding that is enormously beneficial to testing the vision of the piece through empirical input. Working regularly with a company paradoxically gives the single-vision outsider a family and home in which to accomplish the crucial collaborative work and deliver the piece to an audience.

Shakespeare, Molière, and Chekov all collaborated with established companies in creating new work. *Nicholas Nickleby, The Grapes of Wrath, The Cockfighter,* and *Enough* were adapted for specific ensembles. The company members' shared vocabulary, history, and understanding of strengths and weaknesses could guide the adaptor to test ideas and adaptation strategies.

Several notable modern productions have employed the adaptor as director, and some of these auteurs have focused a great deal of their work on literary adaptation. Frank Galati, whose Steinbeck adaptation I have explored in some depth in this book, is an auteur who has also written and produced well-received and adventurous adaptations of the work of William Faulkner and Gertrude Stein. And the following contemporary auteurs have brought breathtaking insight to the dual roles of adaptor and director of new works based on literature.

NEIL BARTLETT: A playwright, adaptor, director, translator, and novelist. Bartlett was also the artistic director of London's Lyric Hammersmith from 1994 to 2004. There he adapted and directed several texts by Balzac, Dumas, Wilde, and Dickens, in the company's small space and on limited budgets. His *Christmas Carol* required only eight actors and a lightbulb. His 2007 adaptation of *Oliver Twist* played London and New York using an evocative stageable image of penny-dreadful machines: spooky, glass-fronted boxes that animate when a coin is slotted in, bringing to life miniature mechanical tableaux of hauntings, crimes, and lurid titillations. He also employed the look of Madame Tussauds–style waxworks and nineteenth-century design conventions, including footlights, two-dimensional scenery, and fly-ropes.

PETER BROOK: Founder of the International Centre for Theatre Research. *The Man Who* is his adaptation of Oliver Sacks's book on neurological problems, *The Man Who Mistook His Wife for a Hat*. Brook's stinging visual metaphor was a hospital-like setting on a bare stage. The costumes, set, and blocking—three men wearing white doctors' jackets walking around white chairs—enriched the visual metaphor of the clinical setting, in which the actors could switch from playing doctors to playing patients. The acting style, which Brook developed with a core group of international actors who were his regular collaborators, focused on a sense of *being* rather than *performing* on stage. Brook and the actors did additional research in mental hospitals and forged an adaptation that built on the theme of what it is to be human.

Brook worked for a decade to adapt for the stage *The Mahabharata*, an ancient Hindu poem fifteen times the length of the Bible. To adapt it he focused on creating characters in dramatic action that could sustain the archetypes from the myths, legends, folklore, history, tales of war, and theology of ancient India. The staging image incorporated repeated use of real fire, water, and earth. It was staged for the Avignon Festival on tons of yellow sand and a pond set in a limestone quarry with audiences on scaffolding.

FRANK CASTORF: An innovative adaptor-director who, as artistic director of the seminal Berliner Volksbühne Theatre, shapes his material with one of the world's leading ensembles. His methodology often involves a long rehearsal process of working through a novel chapter by chapter while editing, improvising, and inserting other theoretical texts that conjure the intellectually provocative social satire he seeks. Other conventions he employs in his theatrical mix are film and video footage, loud music, and playful slapstick. When Sally MacGrane interviewed Castorf in January 2007 for the *New York Times,* he called his adaptation style "piratery—marauding for aesthetic snapshots." Usually only a fraction of the original text remains in his productions, a style that has his critics calling him the "text wrecker." His sources include Dostoyevsky, Pitigrilli, and even Hans Christian Andersen's "The Snow Queen."

MOISES KAUFMAN: An Argentinian-born graduate of New York University's Experimental Theater Wing. The source material for his adaptation of *The Three Trials of Oscar Wilde* came from the extant trial transcripts of the infamous Wilde trials. In conceiving the work for the stage, he chose an evocative stageable image of a skeletal courtroom defined primarily by long tables. The movable tables allowed him flexibility in shifting the action and thus suggesting the overlapping drama of these trials. The success of the Wilde piece allowed Kaufman to create his Tectonic Theater Project: a company of actors, designers, and dramaturgs who went on to collectively create stunning pieces such as *The Laramie Project,* a work adapted from interviews in Laramie, Wyoming, with local citizens affected by the vicious murder of a gay college student.

EMILY MANN: A renowned adaptor of literary sources and the artistic director, for two decades, at the McCarter Theater at Princeton University. She is best known for her documentary style and states her goal as "The recovery of historic memory. It encapsulates why I began and why I continue to write my plays." Her documentary approach to theater and texts guided the construction of several works, including *Having Our Say, the Story of Two Afro American Centenarian Sisters,* by Sarah and Elizabeth Delany (nominated for a Tony Award for Best Play); *Anulla: An Autobiography from the Words of a Holocaust Survivor;* and texts from the Bay Area murders of Harvey Milk and Mayor George Moscone in her compilation play *Execution of Justice.* She has also adapted and modernized Anton Chekhov's play *The Seagull* into *A Seagull in the Hamptons.*

SIMON MCBURNEY: Artistic director of the British Théâtre de Complicité. He has adapted and directed the Swedish novel *Light* and the French novel *Three Lives of Lucie Cabrol.* His signature is physical ingenuity in performance, a style based partly on the work of Jacques Lecoq, in which a character might walk up a wall, emerge from a pail, or act as a projection screen for personal images.

TIMOTHY MCDONOUGH: An American actor-director-playwright. He was my cofounder for Theater Works in Boston and has been one of my principal collaborators over two decades at Theater Emory in Atlanta. His adaptations sustain a signature style of brilliantly constructed works for actors. He adapted Michael Ondaatje's *Coming through Slaughter* and led the script development of our adaptation of *The Collected Works of Billy the Kid.* He also cocreated adaptations based on the anthropological investigation of American families by Jules Henry and John Berger's nonfiction account of peasant life in *Once in Europa,* coadapted with Janice Akers for Theater Emory. His understanding of the transformational abilities of actors allows the audience to make intuitive connections in his delicate, mature handling of narrative.

PAUL SILLS: An American pioneer in both improvisational and narrative theater styles. His mother, Viola Spolin, wrote the definitive book *Improvisation for the Theater,* which was based on hundreds of techniques she developed in improvisation work with professional actors, nonactors, and children. Paul Sills followed up his own development of improvisation by founding the Second City Company in Chicago in 1959. As the leader of a talented group of strong fellow collaborators, Sills simultaneously put his stamp on a style of work and yet relinquished control of aspects of the process to his fellow ensemble members through the improvisational process that was the hallmark of his method.

In 1969 Sills cofounded Body Politic, a company devoted to experiments in narrative, which he and his collaborators called story theater. Their first show, Ovid's *Metamorphoses: Love Lives of the Gods,* combined the narrative of *Metamorphoses* with a fluid, fast-changing improvisational acting style. In 1970 his adaptation of the tales of the Brothers Grimm, titled *Story Theater,* arrived on Broadway, heralding a new style of narrative theater.

Several other companies have followed the lead of Sills's story theater in nurturing a similarly playful style along with respect for the language of the original text to be adapted. Productions such as *Godspell* were an outgrowth of the Story Theater style. Some companies have picked up the story theater work, including the Book It Repertory in Seattle, which is devoted to "transforming great literature into great theater." Its adaptation of *The Cider House Rules* by John Irving played across the country.

ORSON WELLES: Adaptor, actor, director, and producer of theater, film, and radio in the mid–twentieth century. With the actors of their stage company, the Mercury Theatre, Welles and fellow actor John Houseman decided not to simply broadcast the plays they were working on but to focus *Mercury Theatre On the Air*—a weekly hour-long dramatic radio program begun in 1938 on the CBS radio network—on great literature with compelling stories. Welles adapted over thirty famous books for radio. His memorable adaptations of the classics (of which there are still recordings available) include *Heart of Darkness, A Tale of Two Cities, The Magnificent Ambersons, Dracula* (in which Welles played both the Count and Doctor Seward), *Treasure Island, The Count of Monte Cristo, The Thirty-Nine Steps,* and *Huckleberry Finn.* In their infamous adaptation of H. G. Wells's *The War of the Worlds,* the audience was so engaged in the fiction of aliens attacking that panic broke out in several places around the United States.

In radio drama, the text and the oral interpretation are paramount. Welles's greatest adaptor-director innovation in these adaptations was an omnipresent narrator. The narrator might play several roles within the piece. Often he would also play not a neutral storyteller but someone informed, as if he himself were the author.

ROBERT WILSON: An international celebrity who began his work as a physical therapist working with brain-damaged children. He adapted Virginia Woolf's *Orlando,* among several other works, with a theater company in Paris and developed a signature style that includes astonishing visual imagery and glacial pacing. He often storyboards his visual narrative and takes weeks rather than days to tech the lighting and his highly precise blocking. He began working with his own group, The Byrd Hoffman Foundation, and as his technical and performing demands grew he branched out to working regularly with major regional theaters such as Harvard's American Repertory Theater and government-supported theaters in Germany.

MARY ZIMMERMAN: The Lookingglass Theater of Chicago is home base for adaptor-director Mary Zimmerman. She is a former Northwestern University student of Frank Galati, and now, as a professor at Northwestern, she enlists both her students and the Lookingglass Company to help her develop her renowned adaptations, including *Argonautica, The Notebooks of Leonardo da Vinci,* and her Tony-winning *Metamorphoses.*

Metamorphoses sets source material from Ovid around an onstage pool that evokes a Roman atrium, and Zimmerman's staging employs the evocative stageable image of water that both soothes and destroys. She frames the ten chosen myths with the legend of King Midas, interpreted as an uptight dad irritated by his daughter's loud playfulness. He then becomes paralyzed with grief when his newly acquired "golden touch," a gift from the gods, freezes her as he attempts to quiet her. First working with her students and then adding some of them to the Lookingglass Company, Zimmerman had them improvise the Midas scenario, which she set up and then eventually shaped in the writing. Her play exiles Midas until the last scene, when he finds a magic pool that he has been seeking to wash away his now-cursed touch. Freed by the water from his paralyzing gift, he can return to cure his entombed daughter and enact a grateful family reunion.

Models of Collaboration

Some well-established theaters have excellent programs in new play development that offer models for how the collaborative process can work well. Doing some research into the methods and specific techniques that these theaters have used to develop adaptations might be worth your while as you try to envision a workshop process for your own script. The following is a small representative sampling of English-speaking companies whose members create their own literary adaptations in-house or work with outside writers.

1. Actors Theatre of Louisville: The Humana Festival of New American Plays is in its third decade of giving full productions to groundbreaking work. Internationally renowned, this annual festival has included seminal adaptations by Frank Manley, Charles Mee, and Anne Bogart. It has an excellent literary staff that provides dramaturgy and research crucial to the creation of new work.

2. Split Britches, New York City: This troupe's signature style is wild, playful, feminist deconstruction of classics and women's literature. The all-female company plays with Shakespearean gender conventions in reverse, with all roles played by women. Split Britches develops and produces adaptations and new plays with politics and humor as their essential ingredients.

3. Steppenwolf Theatre Company, Chicago: This company commissioned and developed *The Grapes of Wrath*. Its athletic, ensemble-driven acting aesthetic has influenced a generation of actors and adaptors with its "Chicago style." The company's *August: Osage County* received a 2008 Tony Award and a Pulitzer Prize. Its ongoing ensemble provides a strong shared vocabulary for play creation.

4. The Talking Band, New York City: Comprised of former members of Joseph Chaikin's Open Theater, Talking Band works with writers to create highly poetic and often musically informed theater pieces using the body and voice as instruments.

5. Touchstone Theatre, Vancouver: Touchstone has produced plays and developed inspired adaptations for a quarter century. Its work mixes modern Canadian plays, adaptations, and classics in both workshops and full productions. It has wide-ranging connections to the Vancouver Theater community and draws in outside artists and other companies to share new work.

6. Shared Experience, London: This troupe has a long history of adapting nineteenth-century novels that are theme focused and have a signature style in expressive physical theater and dramatic images. Works include Charlotte Brontë's *Jane Eyre* and Leo Tolstoy's *Anna Karenina.*

7. Theater Emory, Atlanta: Since the late 1980s, Theater Emory, where I created several adaptations while Artistic Director from 1989 to 2006, has developed over eighty new works in collaboration with playwrights and adaptors as part of its Brave New Works series. Emphasizing playwrights as the final arbiters of what is written, all the other collaborators follow their lead in the process. During the discussions held after each reading, playwrights are allowed to listen without comment, if they prefer, and let the director or dramaturg mediate, while the collaborators describe what they read, heard, or imagined, and why it works.

Playwriting Centers

Some theaters devote themselves entirely to the development of new plays, including adaptations. Here are a few notable examples of new play centers that are devoted to the creation of new work.

- Sundance Theatre Lab and Theatre Program, Sundance, Utah: This major innovator in script and adaptation development offers resources and collaborators in visual arts, storytelling, clowning, and other disciplines contributing to the imaginative strategy of play construction.
- Wordbridge Play Lab, Clemson, South Carolina: Modeled on Sundance, Wordbridge's focus is on graduate-school playwrights and some undergraduates. Initially housed at Eckert College, it has since moved to Clemson University. A team works on each play for two weeks to challenge the playwright to make the ideas clear and the characters consistent.
- National Playwrights Conference, Waterford, Connecticut: This world-renowned conference at the Eugene O'Neill Theater Center began in 1964 and is dedicated to the development of talented playwrights and their work. Plays by John Guare, Wendy Wasserstein, August Wilson, and many others have been workshopped there before going on to Broadway. Over sixteen hundred manuscripts are submitted and twelve selected to participate in the July conference.
- Playwrights' Center, Minneapolis: Created by a group of playwrights to help develop adventurous new work, this lab has multiple programs,

including residencies, commissions, readings, stagings at the various stages of development, and in-house dramaturgy.

Establishing a Collaborative Relationship with a Theater

So those are some of the heavy hitters—nationally and internationally recognized theaters and playlabs—places that can put serious resources behind you to help you develop your play if they like your work. If you are already a theater professional, you are no doubt familiar with some of the existing programs described here and may know which you would love to work with as you seek to get your adaptation on its feet.

If you decide to approach a theater company about your play, try to gain some experience of its work first. Many theaters are open to good new writing. Reading the season announcements or production histories of the company, you can get a solid sense of its commitment to new work and literary adaptations. Go see shows that the company produces. Attend a workshop, or maybe even volunteer there. If you are a fan of a theater's plays, then helping out as an usher, script reader, or driver will make your contact with the company more personal.

Once you know something about a company's work and style, and, better yet, if its members also know you, present the outline of your adaptation to the literary manager, new play director, a favorite actor, or the artistic director to see if the story engages him or her as well. If it does, the theater could set up a three-to-four-hour workshop for actors to read your scenes and perhaps include a director in the process or make a dramaturg available to you. Depending on the company's artistic mission, in relation to what the members find promising in your script, they might want to do more elaborate work on the piece. You will need to decide how much input is helpful and whether to go forward or not. Whatever happens in a collaborative creation, as the adaptor you should retain the rights to the adaptation so that, at worst, you can walk away with your original draft. At best you will have also gained inspired ideas about character development, how to structure the play, and actions and environments that will activate the words.

And if you are new to theater and looking for ways to realize an idea you have for an adaptation, collaborators may not be hard to find. You certainly needn't start with major regional theaters and national new play programs as you first begin to hone your craft. Creative-minded friends can help you to hear your scripts by reading them aloud. And if you are a student or are involved in a community theater or a writers' group, you may have willing collaborators at the ready to offer you voices for your characters and feedback on your vision.

A Way to Start: The Readers' Theater Model

One model that may prove useful in your first forays into adaptation is that of readers' theater. This style of adaptation from literature privileges the text and expects that the actors will use their scripts for a performance or reading. With text in hand, or on music stands, the readers act what they can with minimal props, costumes, and lighting, and with no scenery. The focus stays on the words, characters, relationships, and conflicts. It is an oral-interpretative event in which voice, gesture, and inhabiting the character quickly allow the audience to imagine where they are and enjoy the story being told.

Readers' theater invites anyone, both the highest-caliber professional actors and a fifth-grade class in an inner city, to adapt virtually any style of literature into bare-bones theater. This physical, visceral access to the text allows storytelling that helps inform the reader and audience of the text's structure, characters, and themes as the players embody and empathize with the characters. The actors also read the story-anchoring details of the descriptive narrative, unfolding for the reader's and audience's imagination the specifics of time and place that reveal the characters. Readers' theater invites a personal, involved, direct experience of the story and characters, which opens up corridors of conversation on a text's intent.

Using the methods of readers' theater, literature can be adapted by almost anyone: a teacher, ensemble of actors, director, playwright, or game student. Orson Welles's Mercury Theatre radio broadcasts were, in essence, high-quality readers' theater adaptations. Without the time-consuming constraints of production values in staging, sets, full costumes, props to be handled, fight calls, and technical elements to balance, a readers' theater script can be rehearsed in a matter of hours and still yield many of the satisfactions that live performance offers.

A remarkable evolution of the readers' theater format is seen in *Gatz*, the much-admired enacted reading of the New York theater company Elevator Repair Service, in which the actors read F. Scott Fitzgerald's seminal American classic, *The Great Gatsby*, word for word, over six hours. The stage setup for *Gatz* uses the surprising yet revealing evocative image of a generic office, complete with obsolete equipment and coffee-stained papers stacked in mountainous drifts. The bleached-out utilitarian color scheme conjures the kind of office where many of us spend much of our lives. An office functionary enters and finds his desktop computer malfunctioning. Waiting for tech support, "Nick" finds a tattered copy of *The Great Gatsby* on his desk and begins to read . . . and read. Others from the office join in as he continues. The office workers first contribute random lines of dialogue that overlap with their office duties, but then they fall more completely into their destined roles: a big-shouldered warehouse type becomes the Ivy League thug Tom Buchanan, and a sexy front-office woman develops into Gatsby's fickle debutante, Daisy.

The reading of *Gatz* surprised the culture at large by becoming one of the critical and popular theatrical hits of 2010. The adaptor was rightly stubborn in taking on the text in a way that most thought impossible. How lucky to be in an industry that allows the seemingly far-fetched and long-reaching to become a reality. And how wonderful to be able to play, especially when extraordinary words are available for adaptation.

My hope is that you will take stock of your resources and find a way to get your work produced. As this survey of approaches to collaboration attests, many models inspire. Use the Internet, your local newspaper, the programs from performances you enjoy, and workshops at a nearby university or community center, and talk to anyone and everyone who might be able to connect you to a vibrant community of theater artists. They can be a valuable sounding board for shaping your adaptation and giving it a full life on the stage.

Appendix

Adaptations by Vincent Murphy

The Lottery, by Shirley Jackson, 1967.

Of Heaven and Hell, from William Blake's *Collected Works,* 1971.

Frogs, by Aristophanes, as part of the company of Medicine Show, 1973.

Murphy's Vaudeville 74, based on multiple sources, 1974.

Electra, from the Greek myth, adapted from the Hoffmannstal libretto, 1976.

Knots, by R. D. Laing, a dance theater event, 1977.

The Collected Works of Billy the Kid, by Michael Ondaatje, with Tim McDonough, 1978.

Enough, by Samuel Beckett, 1979, 1982, 1992.

They All Want to Play Hamlet, based on Shakespeare's *Hamlet,* with Jon Lipsky and Tim McDonough, 1980.

Me and My Shadow, based on "Petition," by John Barth, 1982.

Caligula, by Albert Camus, 1983, 1991.

Pathways to Madness, by Jules Henry, adapted with Tim McDonough and Mark Diamond, 1983, 1985, 1993.

Scheherazade's Sister, by John Barth, adapted with Kirsten Giroux and Kathleen Patrick, 1983.

Out Out, a performance art event based on multiple sources, 1985.

Power Plays, a mime event based on *Monopoly,* 1986.

Bad Water, adapted from the travel journals of Kirsten Giroux, 1987, 1992.

Black Witness, from the novels and essays of James Baldwin, 1988.

Dreaming with an AIDS Patient, by Robert Bosnak, with Jon Lipsky, 1989–90.

Tiempo Libre, from a Greek myth, with Wendy Hammond, 1990.

Little Grey Bushes, from the journals of Athol Fugard, 1991.

The Van Gogh Gallery, based on the art and letters of Vincent van Gogh, 1993.

The Survivor, based on the autobiography of Haing Ngor, with Jon Lipsky, 1994.

The Cockfighter, by Frank Manley, 1998.

The Man Died, by Wole Soyinka, 2000.

1,001 Nights, based on *The Arabian Nights,* 2001.

Crow, by Ted Hughes, 2003.

Bibliography

Barth, John. "Petition." In *Lost in the Funhouse.* New York: Doubleday, 1968.

Beckett, Samuel. *First Love and Other Shorts.* New York: Grove Press, 1974. *

Blake, William. *The Complete Poetry and Prose of William Blake.* New York: Anchor Books, 1965.

Bose Sudip. "Poultry in Motion." *Washington Post,* 10 May 1998.

Brook, Peter. *The Empty Space.* New York: Discus, Avon, 1968.

Chaikin, Joseph. *The Presence of the Actor.* New York: Theater Communications Group, 1972.

Dillon, John. "Paradoxical Professor." *American Theatre* 12 (October 1995), 20–25.

Foote, Horton. "Writing for Film." In *Film and Literature: A Comparative Approach to Adaptation,* edited by Wendell Aycock and Michael Schoenecke, 6–20. Lubbock: Texas Tech University Press, 2004.

Franklin, Nancy. "America, Lost and Found." *New Yorker,* 8 December 2003, 125.

Galati, Frank. *The Grapes of Wrath.* New York : Dramatists Play Service, 1990. *

Greene, Robert. "Greene's Groats-Worth of Wit." London, 1592.

Hulbert, Dan. Review of *Enough. Atlanta Journal Constitution,* 14 May 1998.

Ibsen, Henrik. *Enemy of the People.* New York: Viking Press, 1951.

Manley, Frank. "The Rain of Terror." In *Within the Ribbons.* San Francisco: North Point Press, 1986.

Manley, Frank. *The Cockfighter.* Minneapolis: Coffee House Press, 1998. *

Manley, Frank. *The Evidence.* Atlanta: Playwriting Center of Theater Emory, 1992.

Manley, Frank. *The Rain of Terror.* Atlanta: Susan Hunter Publishing, 1987.

McBurney, Simon. "Quotes." *The European Graduate School.* www.egs.edu/faculty/simon-mcburney/quotes/.

McGrane, Sally. "Outrageousness . . . Frank Castorf." *New York Times,* 14 January 2007.

Murphy, Vincent. *The Cockfighter.* Portland, ME: Smith and Kraus, 1999. *

Oates, Joyce Carol. "Novelist Finds Bare Bones of Play." *New York Times,* 18 November 1990.

Ondaatje, Michael. *The Collected Works of Billy the Kid.* New York: Viking Press, 1974.

Review of *The Cockfighter. Publisher's Weekly,* 26 January 1998.

Spitz, Bob. "The Talented Mr. Minghella: What Liberties Won't He Take Bringing Novels to the Screen?" *Sky,* August 2000, 75–79.

Steinbeck, John. *The Grapes of Wrath.* New York: Viking Press, 1939.

* Used by permission.

Index